D0169975

Divorcing with Dignity

Mediation:
The Sensible Alternative

Tim Emerick-Cayton

Westminster/John Knox Press
Louisville, Kentucky

Scripture quotations marked KJV are from the King James Version of the Bible.

Book design by Drew Stevens

First edition

Published by Westminster/John Knox Press
Louisville, Kentucky

This book is printed on acid-free paper that meets the American National Standards Institute Z39.48 standard. ∞

PRINTED IN THE UNITED STATES OF AMERICA
9 8 7 6 5 4 3 2 1

Library of Congress Cataloging-in-Publication Data

Emerick-Cayton, Tim
  Divorcing with dignity : mediation: the sensible alternative / Tim Emerick-Cayton. — 1st ed.
    p.   cm.
  Includes bibliographical references.
  ISBN 0-664-25226-5 (alk. paper)

  1. Divorce mediation—Religious aspects—Christianity.   I. Title.
BV4012.27.E64   1993
306.89—dc20   93-9309

To Jim and Lucy for life.
To Sher for love.
To Jenny and Michael for laughter.

Contents

Foreword

I first met Tim Emerick-Cayton almost ten years ago. At the time, Tim was one of only a handful of pastors who recognized the importance of divorce mediation as a pastoral ministry and was mediating as part of his ministry. Ten years later, Tim is still one of only a few pastors directly engaged in this work. The church has been a most skittish partner when asked to be involved in any way with divorce. Christians seem as uncomfortable with divorce as Jesus' followers were when he ate with sinners and tax collectors. This is unfortunate, since it means that many people feel isolated and without the support of the church at the time they most need it. So it is good news that Tim Emerick-Cayton's book on divorce mediation is now available to us.

The church has been slow to implement its commitment in this area. When it has acted, it has shown that it can provide important support for those in need. For nine years, I directed the major divorce mediation service in the Chicago area, with sixteen mediators working with us. This service was based in a pastoral counseling center in a church-sponsored hospital. But such examples have been the exception rather than the rule.

I have trained thousands of mediators over the past decade. Most of them were attorneys, social workers, or psychologists. Only a few were pastors or pastoral counselors. Yet this is a point of ministry where the church should be involved: Jesus told us that the dispute resolution process was central to the church's work (Matthew 18). Tim

Emerick-Cayton was one of the pioneers in this area, along with church leaders such as John P. Adams, Ron Kraybill, Speed Leas, and Will Neville, and organizations such as the Mennonite Conciliation Service.

Couples facing divorce will find a helpful introduction to divorce mediation in this book. It will enable them to choose more wisely how they will follow through on their decision to divorce. Just as we have discovered in the past two decades that much of the pain and indignity involved in dying is a product of *how* we allow people to die in our society, so too we are beginning to realize that much of the pain of divorce grows out of *how* we encourage people to divorce.

The divorce mediation movement in the legal arena is analogous to the hospice movement in the medical arena: Each offers a recognition that those involved are facing a crucial time, whether it is directly caring for a dying family member or working out how they will parent their children following divorce.

Tim talks of the importance of forgiveness, love, and reconciliation in divorce, a useful counterbalance to the language of judgment and sin, which has typified for too long the church's response to divorce. At a time when we have over a million divorces a year in our society, mediation offers the church an opportunity to act on its commitment to families and family values. Perhaps the day will come when we don't have to choose between an alienating discourse about sin and judgment or an idealized version of love and reconciliation. I look to the day when we as a community can be accountable for the brokenness, alienation, and unfairness of divorce, while offering hope for a community of justice, dignity, and shalom.

This book is a direct, accessible volume that will answer the questions people ask again and again of mediation: We fight all the time; how can we possibly mediate? Do I need a lawyer? What if it doesn't work out? and so forth.

This volume also helps Christian couples facing divorce to consider mediation as a vehicle to live out their faith commitments at a time of testing. I welcome Tim's statement that at the time of divorce, the church needs to be lifting up grace, compassion, reconciliation, and forgiveness, rather than simply sin and judgment. Such support is imperative, because at the time of divorce itself it is difficult to realize forgiveness and reconciliation. And in the face of the many concerns about the impoverishment of women and children at the time of divorce and our social failure to provide child support in single-parent homes, it is crucial as well for the church to renew its commitment to justice and fairness.

Two final thoughts may be in order. In a book that explicitly addresses those identifying with the Christian faith community, it may be important to note that the answer to the question of chapter 7, "What does the Spirit have to do with mediation?" is broader than a denominational label. Indeed, within the mediation community it is intriguing to note how many people who do not directly identify with the Christian community nonetheless find spirituality an important dimension of mediation. As Tim puts it, "Mediation enables the expression of the highest of human values: respect, caring, acceptance, forgiveness, understanding, openness, gentleness, and compassion."

It would also be apropos, in a book recommending divorce mediation, to issue the caveat that this forum is not always appropriate for everyone. Domestic violence in families, for example, may preclude the use of mediation as a truly voluntary procedure. In such situations, mediation often cannot provide a truly safe place for freely chosen decisions to be made. But for those who choose to use mediation as a way to accomplish divorce, the concluding words of this book capture the combination of ideals and realism that is mediation: Mediation does not celebrate the divorce, nor does it lament the demise of the marriage. Mediation provides a way of getting through the divorce so that the divorcing couple will have a better chance of finding the happiness they seek and experiencing the dignity they deserve.

CARL D. SCHNEIDER, PH.D.
Co-Director, Divorce Mediation Institute
Stone Mountain, Georgia

Preface

Divorce is difficult. I know. I've been through it. I've felt the anger, pain, and rejection that divorce brings. It took me several years before I could even think of remarriage. Divorce is not easy, no matter how strong one's faith or self-understanding.

To my second marriage I brought many of the personal issues that caused the failure of the first marriage, particularly those having to do with feelings of unresolved anger left over from childhood. During the past thirteen years my second wife and I have knocked at divorce's door on more than one occasion but have been able to work through the stresses to resolution. I know that many couples have not been able to do so and find that divorce is the best option. *Divorcing with Dignity* is written with the intent of offering them both hope and encouragement.

Writing this book has been part of a long journey that took me from Portland, Oregon (college), to Upper Volta, West Africa (Peace Corps), to Paris, France (studying law), to Washington, D.C. (more study of law and legal work for the government), to San Francisco (seminary), where I now reside. While living and pastoring a church in Marin County, California, I became fascinated with the idea of resolving conflict outside the adversarial-based court system. This interest became acute during studies for the Doctor of Ministry program, and, pushed by friend and mentor Walt Davis, director of the degree program, I was led to the discovery of the newly emerging practice of mediation.

Grasped by the Spirit, I took the leap of faith and moved from parish pastor to full-time divorce mediator. That day, my concept of "pastoral mediation" was given birth, a personal focus that encourages the inclusion of religious values within the mediation process.

During the preceding eight years I have assisted hundreds of couples in untying the knot with as much dignity and grace as we could, together, muster. Each couple taught me something new, because each couple was entirely unique in their approach to that transition. Some couples showed the grace of pure sainthood, giving me the chance to observe just how friendly a divorce can, at times, be. Others challenged me, each other, and the process to the bitter end, spewing anger, hostility, and pain on anyone within shouting distance, including me. I thank them all, however, for they have given birth to this book.

Standing alongside me throughout this career experiment has been my ever-supportive wife, Sher, to whom I give great thanks and to whom I dedicate this book. Frustrated at times with me as a person, she never questioned or challenged my calling to this type of ministry. Sher, here's one instance where I followed my heart.

Equally understanding and supportive have been my parents and in-laws, who supported us during those first tentative months. I owe you all so much, and the check's in the mail.

When the possibility of this book emerged I got nothing but support from Davis Perkins, then editorial director of Westminster/John Knox Press and now director of the press, and lots of help and guidance from Alexa Smith. Thanks for all you have done. Jeri Marler, editor par excellence and published author herself, took my mere scribblings and made them words that, we both hope, will have meaning for you.

Ultimately, it has been the church family that has counted for the success of this new approach to divorce. Colleagues and friends have referred, supported, encouraged, and prayed for me and my ministry, blessing me in ways they may never fully know. I think the church, in the broadest sense, understands that mediation is not a form of encouraging divorce but a caring response to its presence among us.

Divorcing with Dignity is a small way of passing on to divorcing couples a bit of the grace that has been given to me throughout these past ten years. I pray it will affirm the worth of those who read it and help preserve the dignity that God has given all of us.

Introduction

In the 1970s, people began divorcing in a new way. This new approach is called mediation—the use of a neutral third party to assist divorcing couples and families in reaching mutual agreement on all divorce-related issues, thus avoiding the adversity normally associated with divorce. This new approach is designed to preserve values that the traditional adversarial process tends to undermine.

The book is intended to provide an easy-to-read description of divorce mediation drawn from ten years of experience as a divorce mediator. The explanations are purposefully direct, simple, and heavily illustrated so as to be readable to as many people as possible. The level of pain experienced by those going through divorce is too high to do anything other than speak as directly to the subject as possible.

Harold Berman of Harvard University once said that the existing legal structure "frustrates the realization of the virtues it proclaims" (Berman 1974, 40). Because so many people have found Berman's claim to be true, especially with divorce, this book is intended to provide the reader with an understanding of mediation as an alternative to the traditional, adversarial approach to divorce and separation. If you are thinking of or experiencing divorce, I hope you will consider using the mediation alternative, seeking assistance from your own pastor or a referral to a pastoral or nonpastoral divorce mediator.

If you are a professional in the religious, mental health, or legal fields, I hope you will see the value of mediation and add mediators to your list of referrals. Perhaps you will be interested enough to seek the training necessary to do mediation in the context of your own ministry or professional practice.

During the course of my mediation practice I have seen many couples work through deeply felt anger and pain to resolve divorce-related problems with respect, compassion, and understanding. At the end of mediation sessions in which couples have treated each other with generosity and compassion I have often wondered how two people could get along so well and still be choosing to divorce. I then realized that hate and vengeance are not the flipside of diminished love: Two people can still care deeply for each other but no longer share the kind of intimate love that forms the foundation of a happy marriage.

The case illustrations presented in this book do not represent particular individuals or couples. Rather, they are composites, formed from the hundreds of divorcing couples I have worked with over the past ten years.

Lest the reader be left with the impression that to choose mediation means that divorce becomes easy, let me be clear that nothing, even mediation, can accomplish that. Divorce is heartrending. The decision to divorce is one of the most difficult decisions a person can make. Its pain has been characterized by some as equal only to the death of a loved one.

What mediation offers is not a way of preventing the wounds of divorce but a means of approaching divorce that permits the couple to stop the bleeding, apply a degree of healing balm, and minimize unnecessary aggravation. I have often left mediation sessions amazed at how caring divorcing couples have been as they have struggled to reach a mutually agreeable understanding. At other times, I've returned home totally drained, having spent much of my time containing anger's bitter expression or struggling to reach agreement. But in almost all cases, I felt that the couple had regained a bit of their dignity and self-worth.

I often empathized with my client's pain. In their broken relationships I sometimes saw the weaknesses of my own marriage, painful reminders of how fragile marriage can be. More often than not, however, what I experienced was deep sadness. I felt sadness at the loss each had undergone: the despair so visible on their faces, the tension hanging in the air like a heavy blanket. There were almost never moments of great joy because, in most cases, the best that could be achieved was a civilly reached agreement. But there was, and is, a deep satisfaction that the best that was possible had been achieved. Being this intimately involved in the emotional, spiritual, and practical aspects of divorce through mediation is both rewarding and difficult.

While applauding this new way of dealing with divorce, *Divorcing with Dignity* goes another step and describes an approach to mediation from a pastoral and spiritual perspective, an approach that highlights values perhaps not addressed in other approaches to mediation. In my own practice, which I describe as "pastoral mediation," religious and spiritual values are included throughout the mediation process as a way of helping couples and families survive the divorce transition with as much dignity and sense of self-worth as possible. As a "pastoral" mediator I seek to declare God's grace in word and deed, encouraging the couple to express the highest values possible in the midst of conflicting feelings, and minister to each of the divorcing spouses without judgment.

Finding a mediator who can help you deal with spiritual concerns may be difficult. Begin by asking your pastor or spiritual counselor. He or she may have the name of a mediator in your area with such training. If your pastor does not have a referral, contact other clergy to see if they might have a mediator to recommend. If these approaches are not successful, then contact one of the mediation organizations listed in the back of this book and see if it has someone in your area who would be considered a pastoral mediator.

It may be that you will not be able to locate a mediator with specialized training either as a pastor or a pastoral counselor. In that case, explore with the mediators you interview their feelings about issues related to spirituality. Perhaps you will find a mediator who, while sensitive to pastoral issues, would not, or has not, identified herself or himself as a pastoral mediator.

The chapters of this book are designed to answer those questions most frequently asked about mediation. Chapter 1 describes mediation and introduces several couples who have untied the marriage knot using mediation. Their stories help illustrate the method of mediation and its approach.

Many divorcing spouses feel torn between the need to protect themselves by fighting tooth and nail, and the hope that their divorce can be accomplished with minimal pain and animosity. Chapter 2 discusses things to consider when deciding whether or not to mediate, including what family and friends want you to do, and the fears that arise in any divorce. In this chapter, individuals and couples are asked to carefully consider what they want for their relationship and family after the divorce.

Chapter 3 describes a typical mediation by following one couple's experience. This chapter also includes a simple self-test for measuring the possibility of successful mediation.

Chapter 4 is devoted to answering the questions that most divorcing couples ask in the first mediation session or when calling to inquire about mediation. The chapter addresses the court's acceptance of mediated agreements in divorce proceedings, the valuable assistance and guidance that can be given by family-law attorneys, and some cost cutting tips on using paralegal services or doing your own divorce.

Chapter 5 talks about the children. In many cases, the health and welfare of the children is the primary reason divorcing parents use mediation. In fact, in California, the state where I have practiced mediation, any divorce that has a child-related dispute must, by law, be mediated. The reader will meet couples who have had to struggle with custody, visitation, and child support issues. Child-related mediation is sometimes the most difficult type to work through, but the winners are the children themselves when such matters are mediated rather than litigated.

Before beginning mediation, many couples wonder what will happen if mediation breaks down, what alternatives there may be at that point. Chapter 6 anticipates many of these what-if questions and discusses failure to reach agreement, as well as arbitration, mini-court or private judicial options, and other special circumstances that can arise during mediation.

Although spiritual issues are mentioned in other chapters, chapter 7 explores these issues and argues the benefit of mediation over the traditional adversarial approach in helping to express religious and ethical values. I am unabashedly biased in favor of mediation as opposed to an adversarial divorce. This slant shows itself not only in this chapter but throughout the book. While nothing is guaranteed when it comes to divorce, the possibility of a couple or family experiencing some sense of reconciliation, maintaining some relationship, and preserving some dignity and spiritual awareness is far more likely with mediation.

A caution must be added here about my use of the term "reconciliation" in chapter 7 and elsewhere in the book. I use "reconciliation" to mean coming to terms with the divorce itself and learning to show respect for your divorcing spouse. When I describe mediation as a ministry of reconciliation, therefore, I mean that it offers couples an opportunity to move toward mutual respect at the same time as they work to reach agreement on practical matters. By lifting up reconciliation as one of the essential values of pastoral mediation, I do not mean to suggest that mediation is a means to "save" the marriage. That is the work of the pastoral counselor or marriage therapist. Furthermore, due to the pain of divorce, I recognize that striving for mutual respect may be, for even the most devout of Christian couples, beyond the pale and that the goals of justice and fairness may be of first priority during the mediation process. Feeling that one has achieved a degree of either may well provide the first step toward regaining trust and respect.

Finally, chapter 8 gives some helpful tips on getting started in mediation. This is, for some, the hardest part. By following the suggestions in chapter 8, readers can achieve a greater chance for successful mediation, as well as learn ways to include a reluctant spouse.

Divorcing with Dignity is not intended to replace consultation with legal counsel or with professional mediators. Couples are encouraged to get advice and direction from trained and licensed attorneys and talk with trained mediators concerning the specific circumstances of their case. Nothing can replace the training, education, and experience of the professional. Since each state's family law procedures and statutes are different, divorcing couples are strongly advised to seek legal counsel throughout the mediation process. My training and practice in law did not involve me in court-related processes, and I report only what I have learned about legal issues as a mediator.

It is my hope that the reader of *Divorcing with Dignity* not only will come to know more about divorce mediation but also will be reacquainted with the Spirit that permits the human soul to express compassion and understanding even in the midst of great pain and sorrow. When this Spirit is included in the divorce process, the divorce—while emotionally painful—need not be spiritually damaging.

Chapter 1

What Is Divorce Mediation?

Divorce hurts. Feelings of anger can simmer for years. The sense of rejection can linger into new relationships. For many people, the greatest agony of divorce can be the loss of self-respect.

Faced with unrelenting anger and fear, many divorcing people are dismayed at the ease with which they abandon deeply held values such as respect, compassion, and empathy. The desire to hurt replaces what was once intense and abiding love. Revenge supplants caring. Aggression overrides civility. When these and other values are no longer expressed, self-respect and dignity are soon sacrificed.

For many divorcing couples, however, self-respect, compassion, and dignity are being preserved through a new approach to divorce called mediation.

Evan and Nancy: Divorce Made Easier

Evan and Nancy had been married for years when they confronted the fact that they had long ago lost closeness and intimacy as a couple. Painful as it was to end their long marriage, each knew that staying together was no longer possible. Yet in spite of the distance between them and their decision to divorce, they wanted to retain their respect for each other, not only because each genuinely cared for the other but because each cherished the relationship the other had with their children and wanted this closeness preserved.

Fearing the cost and effect of the adversarial process, Evan and Nancy delayed action on their divorce for months.

Then Evan noticed a newspaper article describing the benefits of divorce mediation. After an initial phone conversation with a mediator, they scheduled an appointment. During their first two mediation sessions, Evan and Nancy reached agreement on the distribution of all their property, pension benefits, spousal support, custody and support of their minor child, and college costs for their older child.

Because Evan and Nancy had been anticipating the separation for a long time, they had each worked through the feelings of anger and fear most commonly associated with the transition to divorce, and they had arrived at the sadness of acceptance. Our mediation sessions were characterized, therefore, by neither heated conflict nor raging anger, as so often is the case, but rather by the deep sadness each expressed over the loss of such a long marriage. Each had spent a good deal of time struggling to understand what God was doing in their lives.

Evan and Nancy's decision to divorce was reached in their home; the divorce itself was accomplished in the mediator's office. Although a degree of sadness remains and most likely always will, Evan and Nancy celebrate family events together and are able to talk together about many things, a testimony to the relationship they have been able to maintain and the dignity with which they accomplished their divorce.

Breaking from Tradition: Mediation Defined

During a workshop on mediation at a church-sponsored conference, one woman began by asking, "Why don't they just call it prayer?" Amusing as it is to realize she had confused mediation with meditation, her question highlights how unknown this approach is to many people today.

Divorce has traditionally been associated with the kind of hostility portrayed in such box-office successes as *War of the Roses* and *Kramer vs. Kramer*, as well as TV's "Divorce Court" and "Civil Wars." This traditional approach is adversarial in nature, often leading to intense hostility, expensive court maneuvering and a reduced amount of communication between the parties. It assumes that each party to a divorce has an "L.A. Law" type of lawyer, that only the lawyers talk to each other—and that in an equally hostile fashion—and that the couples, upset and aggravated, stand anxiously by while the battle rages.

Many have found that in spite of initial good intentions, the adversarial approach complicated their divorce by turning small issues into large and complicated problems requiring a great deal of time and money to resolve. This experience has left many feeling victimized, unfairly treated, and a traitor to their values.

While necessary for some, not all couples need or want this kind of divorce. Mediation offers an alternative. Using a specially trained neutral professional to help them, couples can now reach agreement on divorce-related issues without the fallout of an adversarial approach. The mediator provides the couple with legal and financial information, help in understanding the psychological and emotional aspects of divorce and its impact on children and family, and conflict management skills. The mediator judges neither spouse concerning the reasons or motivations for the divorce and remains neutral throughout the process. The pastoral mediator, in addition, may find appropriate opportunities to identify spiritual and ethical values and assist the couple in expressing these values in the decision they make. The mediator's methods are designed to reduce hostility, enhance communication, and encourage the maintenance and expression of respect and caring between the couple and their family. Couples need no longer fear that an end to their marriage will mean an end to their self-respect and dignity. Divorce need no longer be synonymous with tragedy.

During divorce mediation, couples decide for themselves how, when, and under what conditions their divorce will occur. Divorce mediation is time-limited, goal-oriented, and agreement-focused. It is intended neither to save or improve a troubled marriage, like marriage counseling, nor to make decisions for a divorcing couple, such as occurs in arbitration. Rather, it provides the guidance and the environment for couples to reach agreement on divorce-related issues, to put those agreements in writing, and thus, to begin the process of moving into the future.

In most cases, using mediation reduces the cost of divorce. This was first reported by Jessica Pearsons and Nancy Thoennes in 1982. In 1990, after an exhaustive study, Joan B. Kelly reported, "Couples obtaining divorces using the two-attorney adversarial process spent 134 percent more in total fees than couples using a comprehensive divorce mediation to resolve all issues" (Kelly 1990, 15). Pearsons and Thoennes also found that mediation reduced hostility, increased couple satisfaction, and increased compliance with the mediated agreements (Pearson and Thoennes 1982, 28–32).

Ed and Jean: Mediating in the Presence of Anger

Despite several attempts at couple counseling and ongoing individual therapy, Jean and Ed still had an unhappy marriage. Ed was, according to Jean, a dry alcoholic. Although he had not drunk for several years, he exhibited all the classic behavior of an alcoholic, including anger, rage, resentment, and combativeness. For years they discussed the possibility of separation or divorce. Finally, Jean decided to end the marriage.

Ed was very unhappy with Jean's decision to divorce. He grew increasingly angry and unforgiving, demanding and abusive. Jean, on the other hand, having made her decision, felt relieved and excited when she started building a life without Ed. She particularly resented Ed's resistance and hostility whenever they would approach matters having to do with separating.

During their marriage both Ed and Jean had been fully aware of the family finances. There had been no secrets. Each had a well-paying job and felt equal to the other in family decision making. Since Jean's decision to divorce, however, what little trust they had had disappeared. They began to feel caught between their desire to avoid a costly battle and their hostility and anger. The couple felt that if they proceeded, motivated by distrust, they would end up at war and lose what little savings they had built up, but if they proceeded on without guidance, they would not be treated fairly by the other. They were particularly worried about the impact of their divorce on their two young children and the relationship each had with them.

After an introductory consultation, Ed and Jean decided to use mediation. However, Ed's raging anger erupted regularly and repeatedly stalled the process. He would jump up from his chair, shout angrily how unfair this divorce was to him, and charge out of the mediation room.

Time and again, Ed returned. Each time he came back, the mediator would accept him without judgment, acknowledge his anger, and direct the conversation toward completing the agreement.

Ed began to learn that he could reveal his anger and disappointment and stay in the room. This took great patience on the part of both the mediator and Jean. It slowed the process considerably, because it required that the issue at hand be temporarily put aside while Ed raged. Eventually, Ed and Jean reached a point where Ed would say, "Well, I don't have any other choice," and thereby signal his acceptance of the situation. Until the mediator resolved that this was the only way that Ed would ever reach agreement with Jean, the mediator constantly told Ed that he did have a choice and that he could say yes or no. But Ed's anger was too much for him to handle, and his

"I don't have any other choice" was the best that he could do.

It took Ed and Jean five mediation sessions to conclude all matters having to do with their divorce. They fought over the division of the equity in their house, Ed's pension plan, and their mutual debts. At the end, Jean was sure that, reluctant as he may be, Ed would comply with the agreement. Jean knew, for all of Ed's anger, he was, deep inside, an honest person.

Ed and Jean now have nothing more than a working relationship. Divorce mediation did not make them friends. They do talk once in a while about the children and keep in touch about child support. Their relationship probably would not be much different today had they used the adversarial process, but they seemed to find something affirming about themselves as they stuck with mediation to the end and found some consolation in the fact that they saved several thousand dollars along the way. This may be a small consolation for Ed and Jean, who spent so much time working through their anger, but when it comes to divorce, sometimes even the smallest victories can have far-reaching benefits.

Managing Conflict

One of the unique benefits of the mediation process is the way in which emotions are acknowledged without being allowed to block or hinder the goal of reaching agreement. All too often, divorcing couples who use the traditional approach find that their anger is fueled by the adversarial process, and they begin to focus exclusively on their disagreements, losing sight of the things on which they agree. The value of mediation is that such feelings as anger, fear, and rejection can be expressed in a neutral, controlled environment where they can be interpreted and handled in a manner that permits their expression but reduces the likelihood of these emotions being misunderstood and causing an escalation of conflict. This fact, more than any other, most distinguishes mediation from other approaches to divorce.

Karen and Jack: Mediating Only for Agreement

Despite a modest income, Karen and Jack enjoyed their life aboard a houseboat in a waterfront community near a large city. But after just a few years of marriage, their relationship soured, and Karen wanted out. Jack was stubborn and tenacious, accustomed to fighting for his corner of the world. The houseboat represented his goal of living a leisurely life without the stress of earning a high income. And Jack was not about to give it up.

When Karen decided to seek a divorce, she looked for a way to deal with Jack's tenacity. She had seen him in action before and knew that trying to divide their property, which was primarily wrapped up in the houseboat, would be like pulling teeth. She also knew that were she to hire an aggressive lawyer, she would have a long and difficult battle.

Karen heard about mediation through a friend. She was apprehensive at first, fearing that Jack's anger would completely control the process. However, as she thought about an adversarial alternative, she decided mediation would be worth a try.

Karen had not misjudged Jack. Although it was Karen who had spent her own money to purchase the houseboat, Jack insisted that he receive a portion of the equity for his contributions. Whether he would be due this in a court of law was clearly arguable, and Jack admitted this. However, the amount in dispute was not worth the cost of going to court, either financially or emotionally.

Over the course of several mediation sessions, Jack and Karen pulled and tugged. Jack claimed his work on the houseboat was worth a certain amount. Karen disagreed. The mediator guided them through a process in which they attempted, as best as possible, to document the work Jack had done. Karen, on the other hand, sought figures on the purchase price of the boat and its present value, and explored with different lending institutions how much she might be able to borrow to pay Jack off.

Finally, after some grueling tug-of-war, Jack and Karen found an amount they could each live with. It was not a complete victory for either. They each compromised to reach agreement. Once that was settled, the rest of the details fell easily into place. They decided to sell the houseboat. Jack would stay on the houseboat, doing repairs and maintenance, until it was sold. Out of the proceeds of the sale, Jack would receive his agreed-upon amount. From Karen's perspective this worked out well. She had someone in the boat who would treat it well and maintain it properly. They agreed to restrict their contact with each other— to avoid angry arguments—and to use the mediator for all their communications.

Karen and Jack filed for and were granted a divorce before the boat was sold. Months later, when a buyer was found for the boat, Karen paid Jack, and they parted for life.

Jack and Karen neither wanted nor needed to maintain a cooperative, respectful life together following divorce. There were no children, and each would develop a life separate and independent of the other. What they wanted was to part simply and easily, with as few complications as possible. By keeping the hostility and costs to a minimum, they were able to make the transition from marriage to divorce with as little pain as possible, allowing each to focus on the future and the separate lives they were beginning to build. Jack and Karen were able to maintain a sense of self-respect and dignity by parting quietly and peacefully.

Mediation for Situations
Other Than Divorce

Although most couples seek mediation for a divorce, an increasing number of couples are turning to mediation to resolve a wide range of family issues, including sibling disputes over a family inheritance, parent-grandparent disagreements, child discipline arguments, and family business disputes. Other couples reach agreements before marrying or separating or resolve one or more issues in a larger divorce dispute through mediation.

In very rare cases, a couple may find that mediation leads to a decision to work on the relationship. In these instances the couple is immediately referred to a professional marriage therapist and only returns to mediation if the reconciliation is incomplete. However, no couple should enter mediation with the idea that it will bring about the salvation of the marriage.

Words of Caution

Mediation does not work for all couples. Experience clearly shows that many couples are unable to reach agreement and must ultimately rely on a judge to make final decisions. As Jay Folberg, dean of the University of San Francisco School of Law and former president of the Academy of Family Mediators, has written, "Mediation is not a panacea, but it is a promising and rational alternative" (Folberg and Taylor 1985, 7). Some couples are not able to reach agreement nor express or live out their deeply held values in the midst of divorce. Mediation cannot make individuals into new persons. Nor can it create feelings and behaviors that have gone undeveloped for years.

If it becomes evident to either the couple or the mediator that agreement is unlikely, the couple can consider a variety of options that tend to be less costly and far more expedient than adversarial litigation. These alternatives—arbitration, private judicial resources, and mini-courts—are discussed later.

Time-Tested Approach

Although new to divorce and family law, mediation is a time-tested approach to conflict resolution. It has been used for years to resolve labor-management and contract disputes. Moreover, it is the primary way many countries outside the United States resolve all disputes (David 1971); indeed, its use is increasing throughout the world (Lemmon 1991).

A divorcing individual may find temporary satisfaction in taking a spouse "to the cleaners," but he or she will learn that the short-term satisfaction is not worth the long-term consequences. Mediation is the most effective way to help divorcing couples reach important and far-reaching decisions while maintaining their sense of humanity. Its success is easily measured in the positive response of those who have used it. Its greatest value, however, cannot be quantified: the sense of respect, compassion, and dignity it engenders. At a time when many lives are damaged by divorce, respect, compassion, and dignity can seem like priceless treasures.

Chapter 2

Is Mediation Right for Me?

One of the most difficult things to do during a divorce is to disregard the urgings of well-meaning friends and family to get the toughest, meanest lawyer around, and to instead consider mediation. Nearly everyone has something to say about how to achieve a divorce. However, because each divorce is unique, well-meaning people can do a great disservice by giving advice that, in many cases, is based on their own divorce experience or stories heard about the divorce of others. Dignity has a far better chance of surviving when a divorcing couple can keep the influences of others to a minimum and focus on how they want their divorce to proceed.

This chapter is directed at those readers thinking about or going through divorce. Mediators, counselors, friends, and family can also benefit from this chapter by imagining (or remembering) what it is like to go through divorce themselves.

Tom's Divorce: The Angry Family Syndrome

Many parents of divorcing couples do not understand or accept the increasing ease with which a divorce can be achieved today. For many of them, divorce is a disgrace. Not long ago people talked in hushed tones about someone who was "divorced" or was a "divorcée." The latter was particularly suspect due to gender bias and the assumed role of women in society.

Many parents of divorcing couples still look for fault in every divorce as a way of expressing their disappointment,

17

sadness, and fear. Tom's mother is typical. In spite of Tom's acknowledged alcoholism, inability to keep a steady job, and unfaithfulness in marriage, his mother was convinced her divorcing son was the victim of a cruel and vindictive wife who should never be allowed the care and custody of their child.

When divorce touches the lives of their adult children, parents can become strong advocates for a "cut 'em off at the knees" or "make the bastard pay" approach, advocating harsh treatment for the offending spouse. Such parents often express their disappointment and pain by placing fault or blame at the feet of one of the spouses. It becomes difficult for these parents to step back from their feelings and view the divorce from the perspective of the divorcing couple or the children. They see the breakup of the marriage as a broken contract, and someone must be punished.

No matter how much the family loves the divorcing son or daughter, their feelings are not the same as those of the one being divorced. It is, therefore, important for divorcing sons and daughters to keep their feelings separate from the feelings of their families of origin. Decisions are best made based on what the divorcing individual or couple wants, not on what someone else thinks ought to be done.

Doug and Margaret, Peg and Grace: The Angry Adult Children Syndrome

Similar to the angry family syndrome is the angry adult child's reaction to divorce. It is common for the adult children of divorcing parents to side with one parent or the other, urging that parent to take a hostile, adversarial approach toward the divorce to teach the other parent a lesson. These adult children may be urging a particular approach on one parent as a way of venting their own anger and pain toward the other parent and may not have the best interests of either parent in mind. Consciously or unconsciously, they may sabotage any possibility of a mediated, non-adversarial divorce.

Since the decision to divorce may come at any age, divorcing couples with adult children (not necessarily adult-*acting* children!) must guard against allowing the anger and pain of the children to become, or to inflame, their own anger and pain. To keep the needs of others separate from one's own needs requires a good deal of emotional and spiritual self-understanding.

When Doug decided to divorce Margaret, their two adult daughters, Peg and Grace, immediately came to Margaret's rescue. Due to Doug's self-acknowledged alcoholism, Peg and Grace had a great deal of anger left over from their childhood. As a result, each was insecure in male relationships and angry that Doug abandoned their mother in the latter years of life. Peg and Grace immediately began talking to their mother about not being able to trust their father, about how he never called his daughters and therefore didn't care about the family, and about how Mom should get the toughest lawyer around to protect herself.

Margaret became trapped by opposing feelings. On the one hand, she wanted to honor Peg and Grace's feelings because she desperately needed their love and support through this divorce transition. On the other hand, in spite of Doug's alcoholism, she had always trusted Doug to take care of her and believed, deep in her heart, that he would not let her down even now. These conflicting emotions left Margaret paralyzed, and eventually mediation between Margaret and Doug broke down and their divorce had to be settled in court.

Although Peg and Grace were included in two mediation sessions, their desire to see their father punished did not diminish. Certainly, their influence on Margaret was not the only factor contributing to Doug and Margaret's inability to reach a mediated agreement, but it contributed significantly to the distrust that grew as the weeks went by.

Morgan and Burt: The Divorced Friend Syndrome

As the number of marriages ending in divorce rises, more and more of the people around you have divorce experiences. You will hear stories of atrocious settlements, abandoned families, and cutthroat proceedings as in the television show "Divorce Court."

Because mediation has become an acceptable alternative only within the past decade, most divorced people will have experienced only the traditional adversarial process. In many cases, this adversarial approach aggravated conflict and caused hurt feelings. Today, divorcing couples have more options than their predecessors did and can save themselves great emotional and economic stress by not letting the experiences of others influence their approach to divorce. Combatting the fears that are either created or encouraged by others takes great strength and a constant focus on the higher objectives.

When Morgan and Burt chose mediation, Morgan admitted it was hard to resist the urge to "take him to the cleaners." Several of her closest friends had gone through divorce themselves and had told her stories about getting low support payments, about a husband who had run off with the company secretary and the savings account, or about parents stealing children from one another. But Morgan said she wanted to trust Burt and had no reason not to. Although they had grown apart, he had, to her knowledge, never cheated on her, had faithfully brought his paycheck home, had spent quality time with the children, and had kept Morgan up-to-date on their family finances. All the same, Morgan was scared, and while all the blame for her increasing distrust cannot be attributed to her friends, they certainly added fuel to the fire.

Morgan carried this fear with her to mediation. The mediator noticed it immediately and brought these fears into the open. Morgan was given time to express her fears to Burt. Burt, eager to counter with evidence of his trustworthiness, was stopped by the mediator. He was instructed to listen only and to restrain his desire to defend himself. He was told to be a "sponge," absorbing and hearing the fear that Morgan was expressing.

As Morgan described her fears and the stories she had heard, the tension slowly left her body. She became more relaxed, less stressed, and her speech slowed considerably. The mediator gently and in a low tone of voice asked Morgan several questions to get her to describe more fully her concerns. When Morgan finished, the mediator asked Burt to describe what he heard Morgan saying. When Burt responded that he heard Morgan say that in spite of her desire to trust him, she felt fearful because of stories others had told her, there was an immediate change in Morgan. For the first time since they had opted to divorce, Morgan felt that Burt had heard her and understood her. It seemed as if the distrust that had blocked the possibility of mediation was lifted and enough understanding had taken place that they were able to move on to discussing the issues of their divorce.

In that first session and several additional mediation sessions, Morgan and Burt were able to reach agreement on the distribution of their property, the custody of the children, and the amount and length of child and spousal support Burt was going to pay Morgan. Several times during mediation, Morgan revealed that her friends' stories brought back feelings of distrust. But she had learned to work through them to her satisfaction. The end of Burt and Morgan's marriage was not without pain and heartache, but at least they were able to avoid an all-out battle à la the movie *War of the Roses* and take some, perhaps small, steps toward working through their pain and moving forward.

Charles and Holly: Examining One's Fear

The fear associated with the decision to divorce is so powerful that couples sometimes lose the ability to think clearly and begin to imagine the worst things possible. For example, when Holly called me late one night, she was terrified because Charles, her husband, said he wanted a divorce and told her he had "talked to a lawyer." Thinking the worst, she thought he had beaten her to the punch and she would lose her home, her income, and her child.

Holly called me at the recommendation of her pastor. Panicked, she asked for the name of a tough lawyer in her neighborhood. Slowly, I started asking her about her fears and soon discovered that she felt the need to do everything possible to prevent Charles from robbing her of her house, home, and family. By now, Holly's fears had shot through the ceiling.

For nearly an hour, I asked her questions about her fears. What did she think Tom meant when he said he'd talked to a lawyer? Had he talked to one on the telephone? If so, what had he learned? Had he run into a friend or business associate who was a lawyer, possibly not even a family or divorce lawyer, and asked a couple of questions? Could he have been asking questions simply to determine whether he even needed a lawyer? Or had he actually made an appointment and visited with a lawyer? And if so, was it simply to get some information on how to begin the process of divorce, or did he hire that lawyer to represent him?

As Holly answered the questions, she realized that Charles probably had done little more than get information. He probably had not taken any steps toward beginning divorce proceedings. I explained to her the process involved in filing for a divorce, the amount of time it takes, and the fact that she would, by law, receive papers notifying her if Charles had filed any papers, and the lengthy proceedings necessary for a judgment from the court. I explained the many protections the law provides to both parties in a divorce.

Holly's fears lessened as she talked with me, and she began to feel much safer. The call ended with Holly saying she would ask Charles to join her in mediation. A week later they started a process that ended, several months later, in their reaching agreement on all issues and filing for divorce.

In some cases there is legitimate reason to fear the violent response of a spouse. In such cases a good lawyer, a shelter for battered or abused women, and the presence of a close friend are essential. In other words, however, the fears are not based on reality but on worst-case assumptions or the experiences of someone else. These fears can be lessened by talking to a neutral party, a therapist, a pastor, or a friend who is able to remain objective and help you understand the feelings you are experiencing.

Protecting Yourself

Another overwhelming fear during divorce is that an unscrupulous spouse will take all the money and hide it away. Many people ask how to tell if their spouse is hiding money and what can be done about it. Diminishing trust means that spouses do not believe that the other will act responsibly and in fact will do everything possible to financially cripple the other.

The fact is that the chances of such a thing happening are slim. Hiding or taking money from a bank or savings account without leaving a clear and traceable paper trail is very difficult. In the worst case, such assets may have to be traced through a detailed accounting.

Bank accounts, stock holdings, investment retirement accounts, and savings plans all carry accurate and detailed records from which it can be determined what happened to the asset at any given moment. If one spouse removes all the money from a bank account, for instance, it is possible to obtain a bank statement that shows how much was withdrawn, when, by whom, and in some instances, where it went. The spouse that removes the money is then required to account for the money during mediation or through the attorneys in a traditional approach. The same is true of other property and assets. Pension plans can not be tampered with without a record of the transaction, and property can not be sold without a record of its sale.

Some divorcing people believe that their spouse will run away and not pay spousal or child support. This is a legitimate fear. The nonpayment of child and spousal support has reached epidemic levels in the United States, prompting many legislative and legal efforts to curb this trend. Legislation is now being considered to make the failure to pay child support a federal crime.

The statistics on mediated divorce, however, show a significant difference from the incidence of nonpayment in non-mediated divorce. One study of child custody mediation found that more than two-thirds of participating spouses using mediation were "highly satisfied" with the mediation; 93 percent said they would mediate again or recommend mediation to a friend. A high percentage of mediated agreements were complied with completely (Pearson and Thoennes 1982, 28–32).

The reasons for satisfaction with mediation seem to relate to the improved communication experienced by the divorcing spouses. Pearson and Thoennes reported that 70 percent of the individuals in successful mediation and 31 percent in unsuccessful cases reported improved communication with their spouse (1982, 28–32). When both parties participate in reaching a decision about spousal and child support, they have put their word on the line, been part of the process in reaching the decision, and established an approach to decision-making that promotes openness and honesty and encourages compliance.

The best ally a divorcing spouse can have during that difficult transition is the ability to communicate with his or her partner. Whatever enhances and promotes that communication will, ultimately, work to benefit you and your children.

Greg and Betty: The Blame Factor

A significant barrier to identifying one's own feelings and goals is blaming your spouse for what seems wrong or hurtful. Pain and anger are both normal and often present in divorcing couples. Blaming the other spouse for the breakdown of the marriage will often lead to unsuccessful mediation. Such was the case of Greg and Betty.

Greg and Betty had been married for nearly twenty-five years. Greg was a workaholic who believed his only role was to provide for the family. Caring for the two children and homemaking was left entirely to Betty. Greg made a good salary, was very successful, and brought the family status and wealth.

Greg and Betty's marriage, however, was distant. The roles they played resulted in little intimacy and many unfulfilled needs. When, as an adult, one of the children accused Greg of sexually molesting her as a child, the marriage erupted. Greg, denying any wrongdoing, moved out and asked for a divorce. They came to mediation because they wanted to avoid the enormous legal costs that would most likely accrue in their case.

Betty was very hurt and had a great deal of legitimate anger. In our first mediation session, Betty said she wanted to continue the marriage but wanted Greg to go to counseling. He refused and professed his innocence. Nearly every discussion during the course of mediation came back to Greg's culpability and, in Betty's eyes, his responsibility to Betty and the family for the remainder of their lifetime.

Although both professed a desire to mediate, the closer they came to agreement, the more Betty's anger and resentment surfaced. After nearly a year of mediation, Betty abruptly terminated mediation and told Greg, via a letter, that her case would now be handled by a lawyer.

Surprisingly, Betty's termination came just when Greg had conceded her every demand, leaving the impression that

Betty had entered mediation with the wrong goals. Perhaps she thought that through mediation, she and Greg would be able to reconcile. Perhaps she thought that the nonadversarial approach would provide an environment for Greg to confess his alleged crime. In any case, neither of these happened, and mediation ended without agreement.

Blame is two-pronged. First, the blaming spouse often paints a picture of the other as totally responsible for the divorce. This picture usually includes a description of the blaming spouse's innocence and surprise. Second, the blaming spouse believes that the guilty spouse must pay—monetarily, emotionally, or in both ways—for the pain and suffering of the family.

Betty entered mediation placing all the blame for the divorce on Greg. Even after months of mediation she was unwilling to soften that position, and it became clear that mediation would not work for this couple.

Working through the blame factor requires quieting the external and internal voices and listening to the voice of the heart. To quiet the raging voices is to work through the need for revenge, punishment, or striking back. Revenge may be sweet, but it leaves the soul with a deep and lasting bitterness. Harbored bitterness, unresolved anger, or festering self-pity can eat away at the human spirit like a cancer. These feelings are best dealt with through appropriate professional therapy. If maintained, such emotions will ultimately sabotage the best mediation efforts.

Christine and Phil: Taking Responsibility for Your Part

Christine didn't want a divorce and was extremely hurt and angry because Phil had fallen out of love with her and in love with someone else. Christine wanted to continue the marriage but eventually came to accept Phil's decision.

When Phil moved out and asked for a divorce, Christine was able to keep her hurt and pain from turning into blame. She knew she was angry, but she did not put all the blame on Phil for the breakdown of the relationship. She realized that the unhappiness and dissatisfaction they experienced in their relationship was as much her responsibility as his. Christine found the strength she needed to accept her role in the breakdown of the marriage through the spiritual disciplines of prayer, meditation, and study. Her response is a perfect example of seeking appropriate support outside the context of mediation.

Because Christine was able to prevent her deeply felt pain from turning into a need to blame Phil, she and Phil were able to effectively use mediation to reach agreement.

The Essence of Mediation—Shared Decision-Making

For mediation to be effective, both parties must be able and willing to exercise decision-making power. While this sounds easy, for many it is difficult.

For some couples, unhealthy decision-making patterns from the marriage carry over into mediation. These problems generally present themselves in one of two forms.

In the first case, a spouse who is accustomed to unilateral decision-making authority will decide, prior to mediation, what should be done with the property and the children, or will make decisions about the amount and length of financial support. Eager to get to the agreement, this type of spouse will propose a complete divorce package (distribution of property, support levels, child custody schedules, and so on) very early in the mediation and will be shocked when that proposal is not accepted without question by the other spouse.

The second form of this problem is represented by the spouse who grew accustomed to the other spouse making unilateral decisions and now, faced with the need to make decisions as a separate person, becomes paralyzed with fear and cannot accept that responsibility. Although the former difficulty is, in my experience, easier to overcome through mediation, either of these unequal styles of decision-making renders mediation difficult at best and often impossible.

The essence of mediation is *shared decision-making*. Both spouses must be willing to set aside old patterns of decision-making and, even if this is a new approach for them, become informed and willing to share the decision-making power in a balanced and equitable way. For some, this means learning to be patient while the other spouse becomes informed enough to be part of the decision-making process. For others, it means coming to accept the fact that they must take responsibility for their future and decrease their dependence on their former spouse.

If equality in decision-making is not present at the start of mediation, it is appropriate for the mediator to help the couple work through this barrier before addressing the issues before them, or to refuse to continue the mediation until the couple has, with professional therapy if necessary, reached a point of equality in decision-making.

Steve and Amy

Steve and Amy, married fifteen years, were in their late thirties when they divorced. They elected to mediate because they had several young children and wanted to maintain as good a working relationship as possible for the sake of the children.

When they were married, Amy became the homemaker after the birth of their children. Steve was the breadwinner and provided for the family to the best of his ability, staying with one employer in spite of deep unhappiness and dissatisfaction with his job. Amy, a talented artist, decorated their home, mothered the children, and did volunteer work in the community.

As the children grew older, Amy wanted to expand her world by going to school or to work. Steve strongly opposed the idea, and Amy stayed at home. Over time, Amy could no longer live with her frustration and unhappiness. After trying to work on the marriage through counseling and couple therapy, she asked Steve for a divorce.

Amy soon learned something surprising about herself. Although she wanted a divorce, she found it extremely difficult to make financial decisions. She wanted independence but was unprepared to deal with the responsibility that accompanied independence.

Steve and Amy nearly ended their mediation on several occasions. Amy was worried, particularly over the amount of spousal and child support they were considering. Twice during mediation, Amy consulted with her advising attorney about this issue. When her lawyer could not advise her about the exact amount she should receive for support, she accused the lawyer of not knowing the law. During mediation, the couple had carefully examined the county support guidelines, calculated support in various ways, and used a support guideline computer program to calculate with as much accuracy as possible the probable support level. But no matter what was done in mediation, nor what information Amy received from her advising attorney, she could not come to grips with the responsibility for her future or reach agreement on the amount of family support. Mediation ended with all but that one issue decided. I heard later that their attorneys had worked out a satisfactory amount and Amy had consented, but only because someone—her attorney in this case—made the decision for her.

Jack and Barbara: Improved Outcome
for Women and Children

In *The Divorce Revolution,* a controversial work disputed
by other studies, Lenore Weitzman reported that women
experience a significant decline in their standard of living
in the first year after the divorce, while their former hus-
bands experience an *increase* in their standard of living
(Weitzman 1985).

For this reason, couples who select a mediated approach
to divorce have an opportunity, if the parties are willing,
to take nontraditional approaches in dealing with the
economic issues in their divorce and thus assuring for
themselves and their children a more equitable outcome.

An essential ingredient in finding more equitable solutions
to the economic problems of divorce is to encourage the
parties to take responsibility not only for their part of the
breakup but for the mediated outcome.

Jack and Barbara were a couple willing to stand by their
decisions. Barbara worked throughout the marriage and had
the confidence that she could make her own way in life. At
the time of their mediated divorce, Jack was making a
career change from self-employed carpenter/contractor to
paramedic.

Both Barbara and Jack accepted responsibility for their financial decisions. When they explored spousal and child
support, each looked carefully at their income or potential
income and at their budget needs and agreed on monthly
support. They were interested in finding a solution that
worked for both of them.

Once divorced, they worked as hard as possible to fulfill
their pledge. When one of them was unable to meet an
obligation, they discussed it and worked to find a solution.
At a time when money was short and needs great, they were

strong enough to accept responsibility for fulfilling each other's, and their children's, needs.

When spouses are willing and able to make decisions and stand by them, their chances of successful mediation increase dramatically. When they are unwilling or unable to make decisions, it is more likely that the mediation will not be successful. Both spouses must be ready to state their needs, negotiate a settlement of those needs, and accept the consequences of those decisions.

It is common for one or both parties to be unprepared to make tough decisions at the outset of mediation. Don't be discouraged. A good mediator can, in most cases, help the less willing, or less able, spouse become stronger in decision-making.

Roberta and Frank

Take the case of Roberta and Frank. During their marriage, Roberta had no responsibility for financial decisions. When Frank asked for a divorce, she was devastated.

Through individual counseling, Roberta was able to accept the fact that the marriage could not be recovered. She then took it upon herself to become knowledgeable in all areas of the family finances. She worked closely with the family accountant, grew increasingly confident in her ability to make sound financial decisions, started looking closely at her property from an investment perspective, looked long and hard at her budget needs, and sought work experience that would lead her to self-reliance.

Her first job was as a receptionist in a professional office. She worked hard, developed her skills, and moved to a better-paying, more secure job that gave her greater satisfaction. Although initially scared to face the future alone, she developed into a strong and capable decision-maker, able to evaluate decisions from a variety of perspectives.

Where You Want to End Is a Clue About Where to Begin

Before beginning mediation it is important to be clear about your expectations for yourself and others after mediation. The goals you have set for yourself will be helpful tools in dealing with your spouse throughout the divorce. If, for instance, you decide that what you want is a clearly stated agreement about child visitation, then having this goal at the beginning of the mediation will help you respond even to issues that are unrelated to visitation but that may be points of negotiation and used in bargaining to reach your goal. Deciding what each spouse wishes things to be like after the divorce is an important element in deciding whether mediation is right for you. Deciding what you want requires

— recognizing the impact of the divorce on your thoughts and feelings
— recognizing that the traditional adversarial approach is based on fear, distrust, and revenge
— examining your own spiritual and personal values to ensure that they are part of the decision-making process.

Divorce is a painful and disruptive experience that turns all of life upside down. During the divorce transition, feelings of anger, vulnerability, and distrust come to the surface. Often, the human reaction is to seek emotional and economic protection as well as assurance that one is still worthy of love. Mediation permits both partners to both give and receive the respect and care they desire.

Respect and dignity are more difficult to maintain using an approach grounded in the belief that, when given the chance, people will behave in a self-serving fashion. My experience mediating hundreds of divorces has convinced me that when given the chance, people usually respond with generosity, cooperation, and caring.

Conclusion

In divorce, as in other areas of life, how individuals act is a reflection of their values. Mediation enables the expression of the highest of human values: respect, caring, acceptance, forgiveness, understanding, openness, gentleness, compassion. All of these and more can be expressed during divorce, even in the presence of anger, fear, and pain.

Keep in mind that when friends urge you to "get a good lawyer" or "take everything you can get," their intentions may be good, but the advice may be bad. Take time to examine with them why they suggest this approach. Then quietly look inside yourself to discover what you want, both now and in the future. It is *your* marriage, *your* divorce, *your* future.

Chapter 3

How Does Mediation Work?

Ted and Pamela met when they were in their thirties. Neither had come close to marriage before. Each was a bit shy and reserved, and also kind, gentle, and intelligent. After marrying, they had a son.

Pamela did not have a significant career outside the home, although she had worked at several jobs before meeting Ted and was good at what she did. Ted was a fire fighter and had been with the department about ten years. Pamela was the primary care parent for Kevin. They attended a neighborhood church where Kevin was baptized, but because of Ted's shyness, Pamela was far more involved and active than was Ted.

As Kevin grew, Pamela became more active in the community and began to find Ted's quietness and lack of communication a great barrier in their relationship. Ted, in spite of personal and couple counseling, was just not able to give Pamela the kind of relationship that would have met her needs. Finally, after a great deal of inner struggle, Ted and Pamela decided to end their marriage.

They talked with their pastor, who told them about mediation, and with friends who had used mediation. Ted and Pamela decided to try it. Their pastor made the referral, and Pamela and Ted each called and talked to the mediator before the first appointment. Let's follow Ted and Pamela through the six months of their mediation.

Step 1: Is Mediation the Right Choice?

Is mediation the right choice? The answer may be no for some couples. Mediation is not a panacea and does not work for everyone. The first step in evaluating this question is to make a reasonable estimate of the chances of success, which requires that the couple reflect seriously on their attitudes and goals.

The following survey (Table 1) helps couples determine whether mediation is a suitable option. Couples should use the survey as a *supplement* to talking with a professional counselor, psychologist, or mediator about whether to try mediation. As I've said to many couples considering mediation, you have nothing to lose by trying. If mediation doesn't work, you can always opt for a litigated, adversarial approach. If it *does* work, you will have saved yourselves a great deal of time and resources . . . and pain.

This simple survey is a beginning point for evaluating the chances of a successful mediation.

The survey raises questions that will help couples evaluate their chances of succeeding at mediation. The higher the score, the more likely they will be able to respect each other's needs and reach agreement. To a great extent, the ability to mediate depends on

— the level of mutual trust
— the balance of knowledge of the spouses
— the level of anger, hostility, or other communication barriers.

The survey confirmed for Ted and Pamela that they still had deep respect for each other, although they agreed that they wanted to end the marriage. Each wanted the other to be actively involved in Kevin's life. Each wanted the other to be secure and happy, and both were willing to go beyond the requirements of the law to see that happen.

Table 1
Is Mediation Right for You?

Answer the following questions on a scale of 1 to 10:

1. Who is to blame for this divorce?   _____
                                      1 (your spouse)–10 (you)

2. How selfish is your spouse?   _____
                                      1 (very)–10 (not at all)

3. How important is money to you?   _____
                                      1 (very)–10 (not at all)

   To your spouse?   _____
                                      1 (very)–10 (not at all)

4. If you have children, who loves them more?   _____
                                      1 (you)–10 (your spouse)

5. When you think of your spouse, what do you wish
   you could do?   _____
                          1 (kill him/her)–10 (make him/her happy)

6. Does your spouse understand your family finances?   _____
                                      1 (no)–10 (completely)

7. Do you understand your family finances?   _____
                                      1 (no)–10 (completely)

8. Is there something that your spouse needs to change
   in order to be mentally healthy?   _____
                                      1 (yes)–10 (no)

9. How much do you have to learn or change about
   yourself in order to be happy in a new relationship? _____
                                      1 (not much)–10 (a great deal)

10. How important is your spouse's happiness to you? _____
   1 (not at all)–10 (very important)

11. Would your spouse intentionally withhold financial
   information in order to pay less support or give you
   less in the division of property? _____
   1 (yes)–10 (no)

12. Will your spouse try to pay as little as possible for
   the support of you or the children? _____
   1 (yes)–10 (no)

13. Are you willing to accept a decrease in your standard
   of living as a result of this divorce? _____
   1 (absolutely not)–10 (if necessary)

14. Will your spouse "win" unless you fight back tooth
   and nail? _____
   1 (yes)–10 (no)

15. Will you be happier if you maintain a respectful
   relationship with your spouse following your divorce, or if you have no relationship with your
   spouse following your divorce? _____
   1 (no relationship)–10 (respectful relationship)

16. Will your spouse be fair with you? _____
   1 (no)–10 (yes)

Total Score: _____

Step 2: Selecting a Mediator

The couple considering mediation should take time and ask questions when selecting a mediator. In the Appendix of this book is a list of professional organizations. The couple might consider contacting one or more of these organizations to confirm that the mediator they are considering is well respected and dependable. Most important, however, is how the couple feels about the mediator they select, because with the mediator's assistance they will be dealing with sensitive and personal decisions.

For mediation to be successful, both spouses must be able to trust that the mediator can provide them with the help they need, both to contain any conflict that may arise and to lead them to agreement. Each spouse must feel comfortable with the mediator's accessibility, competence in areas of divorce information, and general understanding of and approach to mediation.

Step 3: Getting Started and Gathering Initial Information

During their first session together, Ted and Pamela signed an *Agreement to Mediate* and then discussed the process of divorce.

Agreement to Mediate. An Agreement to Mediate specifies the ground rules for the mediation. The agreement Ted and Pamela signed set out clearly the following terms:

— the mediator does not represent either party; rather, the mediator acts as a neutral third party
— any information shared during mediation will not be used in a court of law if a lawsuit arises between the couple
— each party to the mediation agrees to make full and

complete disclosure of information necessary to the mediation process
— the mediator's fees and billing policies are stated.

Ted and Pamela asked about the statement of confidentiality included in the agreement. They were fearful that something either of them said or proposed during mediation might later be used to put them in a bad light in court if they were not able to come to agreement during mediation. Not sure if mediation would be successful, their fears were natural.

It was explained that the Agreement to Mediate adhered to a California law according to which nothing said during the course of mediation could be submitted as evidence in a court of law. Also, it was explained that any document prepared for the purpose of mediation could not be submitted.

It should be noted that not all states protect the confidentiality of the mediation process. Couples should question their mediator about the statutes in their state and understand what can and cannot be used in any subsequent lawsuit.

Their questions answered, Ted and Pamela said they understood the terms and expectations of the agreement and signed it willingly.

The divorce process. I often begin the first mediation session by asking, "Is the marriage really over?" This was an important moment for Ted and Pamela—they had to reflect seriously on the status of their relationship.

Pamela explained that they had been in counseling for many months and that she was certain about her decision to divorce. When Ted started to talk, his eyes filled with tears. It was obvious that he did not want the divorce.

I presented three options for Ted. First, he could fight the divorce by hiring an attorney to resist and complicate the process. This would not only be financially costly, it would also leave them and their child in an emotionally battered state.

Second, he could do nothing, essentially saying to Pamela, "Look, I don't want this divorce. Therefore, you will have to do all the work to get it." This approach would leave him out of the decision-making process altogether.

Third, he could cooperate with Pamela in spite of his feelings, hoping the use of mediation would reduce the pain and hostility of this divorce.

After Ted pleaded with Pamela to change her mind and she remained firm, he agreed to cooperate in the divorce.

Using a flow chart showing the various stages and procedures for a divorce or legal separation, I then described the differences between nonlegal separation, legal separation, and divorce. The chart illustrated the steps involved in getting a legal separation or divorce in their state. Ted and Pamela learned that at any time between the filing of the first court-related paper and the receiving of a final judgment of divorce, they could change their minds, amend the proceedings, delay the proceedings, or get a court judgment even if they had not reached agreement on support, the division of property, and other issues. Ted and Pamela were relieved to know they were not "locked in" once they started the process. They realized they had more options than they initially thought, and the more they learned about the process, the more their tension eased.

While the details of the divorce process differ from state to state, the process generally consists of filing certain documents with the court and submitting a settlement agreement for the court's approval.

Step 4: Separating Agreement from Disagreement

The fourth step in the mediation process is to identify issues upon which the couple agrees or disagrees. Resolving the disagreements comes later.

I began step four with Ted and Pamela by going over a list of items that needed to be addressed during mediation to determine where they agreed and disagreed. Before coming to mediation, Ted and Pamela had started to figure out how they would divide things up, but they ran into issues they didn't know how to resolve, and they realized they did not know all the questions they needed to answer for themselves. They told me what they had been thinking and then asked for help to continue.

Ted and Pamela's questions were typical. They wondered how to divide their house so that Pamela could live there with the children. Neither knew that pension and retirement benefits were considered community property in their state and would, therefore, have to be divided. They had not thought about the fact that their life insurance policies had accrued value during their marriage and needed to be separated. They asked how spousal and child support was to be determined and how long it was to be paid. Ted and Pamela then raised the most frequently asked question: "Do we have to list every single item in the house and its value?"

I answered each of their questions with general information, knowing that as we got further into mediation each issue would be addressed thoroughly by their advisory attorney. Concerning their house, we discussed whether Pamela could "buy Ted out" of his share of the house either with cash or by trading off other assets to him. They might also choose to own the house jointly and calculate a "rental" value to go to Ted because Pamela would remain in the house. We talked about the varieties of retirement benefits and discussed the option that one party could "buy out" the other party after the value of the pension was determined, or the pension could be divided by court order into two separate accounts, giving each party control over his or her portion. Since their life insurance policies were "whole life," I informed Pamela and Ted that the policies would have to be divided equally but that one could buy out the other, or they could cash the policies in and divide the proceeds.

Ted and Pamela discussed spousal and child support, refer-
ring to guidelines published by the superior court in the
county of filing. Ultimately, however, the level and length
of support would either have to be agreed upon by Pamela
and Ted or determined by a judge if they could not reach
agreement. I explained the system of calculation used
for the guidelines and described the many variables they
would have to consider. I knew by experience that
this issue would be initially confusing for Pamela and Ted,
but I assured them that it would become quite clear later
on.

Finally, regarding their many household furnishings, I told
them that the simplest way of dealing with these items was
for them to go through the house and divide things as best
they could. If they had a problem, we could work it out in
another session. I also explained that rather than list all the
furnishings, it was simplest to state in their agreement,
"Household furnishings divided by mutual agreement."
This information seemed to put them at ease. Pamela
turned to Ted and asked if he thought they could do that,
and he said he thought so.

Pamela and Ted completed a worksheet I gave them to help
them list all their property and debts. I explained that they
would have to decide who would take what. Then I asked
them to consider issues of tax liability, Kevin's health
insurance coverage, personal life insurance, college education costs for Kevin, assignment of the income tax exemp-
tion for a child, and issues about the distribution of their
property—a list of issues needing decisions for the final
agreement. At the end of the first session, Ted and Pamela
agreed to think about their areas of disagreement and to
meet again in two weeks.

Step 5: Reaching Agreement

The last step in mediation is to resolve disputes and
achieve consensus. Once the mediator identifies the areas

of disagreement, he or she helps the couple collect the data necessary to thoroughly discuss the issues and assists them in negotiating an agreement.

Pamela and Ted had no idea how to go about dividing property or deciding on child and spousal support or other issues, so I again went over all the issues that required a decision, including child custody, child and spousal support, and division of property.

Child custody. Pamela and Ted knew they both wanted to be involved in parenting and raising their son. In their state, joint legal and physical custody provided them with full involvement as parents. They agreed that Kevin would stay with Pamela most of the time.

Child support and spousal support. Although Ted and Pamela quickly agreed that Ted should pay child support, he did not understand why he had to provide Pamela with spousal support. I explained that spousal support gives Pamela the ability to move from a position of dependence to a position of independence. Realizing that spousal support meant that Pamela would have more time to be the primary parent for Kevin, Ted agreed.

I described how the courts calculate support levels based on the net income of the spouses and the amount of time each had their minor children with them. Based on the available information, their individual budget needs, and their desire to be as respectful of the other as possible, Pamela and Ted arrived at a support level that was acceptable to both.

Property division. Together we looked over their list of property. Pamela had told Ted earlier that she wanted to stay in the family home until Kevin reached school age. They began to look at ways to make that happen. They decided it was important to get an appraisal of the house.

After several hours of mediation, Pamela and Ted grew tired and agreed to another appointment. Each left with a homework assignment: Pamela would get one or more appraisals on the house, and Ted would get current infor-

mation on his pension plan. They agreed to bring the results to the next mediation session.

During their next appointment, Pamela and Ted reached
agreement on the remaining issues, decided who would
prepare the agreement for them, and concluded mediation.
There were still several technical details to be worked out,
including the preparation of a court order dividing Ted's
pension into two parts and the transfer of property title to
Pamela, but these matters would be dealt with by outside
mediation, with an attorney, or by themselves. For Pamela
and Ted, their divorce had required only two mediation
sessions and no court appearance.

Step 6: Filing for Divorce in the Court

When Pamela and Ted heard about the need to file court
forms and to have their agreement written and submitted
to the court, they became confused. It was explained to
them that the court forms were like a tax return that had to
be correctly filled out and filed. Their agreement, on the
other hand, was like a letter that accompanied their tax
form explaining some particular aspect of their reported
finances. Now they understood the difference between the
court forms and the agreement.

It was explained to Ted and Pamela that most couples use
attorneys for the filing of the court form. They also learned of
two additional options available to them. The first was to use
a paralegal service that, for a fee, would complete and mail all
the forms required by the court. The second was to complete
the court-related divorce forms by themselves, using any of a
variety of self-help books available in most bookstores.

However, whether divorcing couples use a paralegal service
or file the court forms themselves, they are strongly advised to consult with a licensed attorney throughout the
divorce process concerning issues of a legal nature or ques-

tions about the rights, duties, and liabilities of the divorcing spouses.

Step 7: Writing the Agreement

Once the couple reaches agreement on all the issues, the agreement must be written up in a form that can be mailed to the court for approval.

Again, although the most common practice is for a couple to have their representative attorney or an independent attorney prepare their agreement for submission to the court, they may also write the agreement themselves using the samples provided in self-help books.

Although preparing the agreement is a relatively simple task, many couples feel better having someone else write it for them, and again, the safest means is to have this done by a licensed attorney.

The recommended way of handling the filing of court-related documents and preparing the agreement for submission is to use a trained and licensed attorney. The process is complicated, and an error may result in unwanted delays or, at worst, unenforceable judgments. Attorneys are familiar with such proceedings and are skilled at seeing that matters are handled correctly.

This advice also extends to consulting with an attorney regularly throughout the mediation. Often a spouse has questions about either his or her rights as an individual or about how the courts would handle a particular matter. An attorney experienced in family law will be in the best position to provide assistance.

Conclusion

To mediate or not to mediate—that is the question. Although not all cases are as simple as Pamela and

Ted's, many couples have used mediation to divorce with dignity.

Will mediation be successful? Only the couple can decide after considering such factors as trust, communication, anger levels, and the ability to put the needs of others— particularly the children—over the needs of self.

Like Pamela and Ted, a couple will never know whether mediation will work unless they try. It is much easier to try mediation *before* using an adversarial approach than it is to stop the adversarial approach after it is under way.

Chapter 4

What About . . . ? Most Frequently Asked Questions

During the different stages of mediation, a number of questions often arise. Because these questions are important, the most frequently asked are addressed in this chapter.

Is Mediation Legal?

Many couples ask, "Is it legal?" They mean: "Does mediation result in a legally binding agreement that is enforceable in court?" The answer is yes, absolutely.

Mediation is a decision-making process applied to the decisions necessary to end a marriage. In any state, and under any circumstances, agreement is permissible under law. Most divorces and other lawsuits are settled by agreement between the opposing parties or the parties' attorneys. Once an agreement is reached, either through mediation or through the traditional process of negotiation between attorneys, the agreement is submitted to the court for approval.

Do We Have to Go to Court?

Many people's understanding of the divorce process comes from watching TV's "Divorce Court" or popular movies about acrimonious divorces. While such adversarial and hard-fought cases really do appear in court on a regular basis, many couples get divorced without such hostility and pain.

In most states, the divorcing couple does not have to appear in court to get a legal separation or divorce, particularly when using mediation. Court appearances are necessary only if the couple cannot reach agreement and a judge is required to render a decision about the custody of the children, the division of property, or some other issue in the divorce. Going to court adds unnecessary expense to the case and tends to highlight or create a sense that the process is an adversarial one.

Can We Mediate Only Specific Issues?

In many instances, couples represented by attorneys will want to mediate one or more of the issues. In fact, in California, if there is a dispute involving the care or custody of the children, that issue must, by law, be mediated before being presented to a judge for resolution. A number of other states have followed California in requiring mandatory mediation for child custody issues.

In other instances, couples represented by attorneys may use a mediator to minimize the hostility or adversarial nature of the divorce while they resolve some or all of the issues, and then have the representative attorneys prepare the court documents.

Reviewing Attorneys or Other Experts

The mediator should direct divorcing couples to have their agreement prepared or reviewed, or both, by independent attorneys for omissions, oversights, or rewording. This is particularly true if the couple prepares the agreement themselves or if the mediator writes a Memorandum of Understanding.

In addition to a lawyer review, there are many occasions when an outside expert is needed. A couple will often consult with an accountant for tax considerations, a real estate agent to work out details concerning the sale of the family residence, or their consulting or reviewing attorney on any legal questions and issues.

At some point during the mediation process, Pamela realized that she did not understand their investments or the tax implications of those investments. After talking about her uncertainty during one of the mediation sessions, she and Ted agreed that she should hire an accountant who specialized in divorce issues. The accountant reviewed tax returns for the preceding five years and explained to Pamela the investments and their tax consequences. Her questions answered, Pamela felt prepared to go on with the mediation.

Due to the extra effort Pamela took in meeting with a specialist, she and Ted were able to reach agreement on all the remaining issues at their next mediation session and process their divorce smoothly and easily.

How Much Does Mediation Cost?

The cost of mediation is usually calculated by the hour. The amount of time involved depends on a variety of factors, including—but not limited to—the ability of the couple to communicate and make decisions, their levels of unresolved anger, and the complexity of the estate. Occasionally, a couple may reach agreement in one session at a cost of only a few hundred dollars; others, for a variety of reasons, spend much more. Although several studies conducted on the cost of mediation have concluded that mediation is generally less expensive than an adversarial approach, the range of those findings, from $1,630 to $3,428, make it difficult to say what the exact cost of a mediated divorce will be (Pearson and Thoennes 1982, 479–524; Kelly 1990, 20).

I have found in my practice that the cost of mediation, including the preparation and filing of the divorce-related papers, ranges from $450 to several thousand dollars. Again, the difference depends on how much the couple do themselves to reduce costs, such as filing or not filing their own papers and writing their own agreement, as well as the degree to which they incorporate attorney consultations into their mediation process.

The cost of a divorce using the traditional two-attorney approach can exceed ten thousand dollars—if there are no arguments or disagreements between the parties (Kelly 1990, 20). There are many cases in which the costs go far higher. With mediation, however, the *couple* controls the cost, since most mediators charge simply for the time spent together. The primary value of mediation is that it gives the couple control over the process.

How Long Does It Take?

Some divorcing couples need only one mediation session to resolve all the issues in their divorce. For many others, however, it takes two or more sessions—sometimes as many as five or ten—to resolve all the issues. The amount of time needed is a function of the number of issues that need to be resolved, the size of the estate being divided, the need to divide pension or retirement benefits, and the couple's ability to communicate and solve differences, as well as the need to use outside consultants or advisers.

What Is Unique About the Mediation Alternative?

Mediation is unlike any other process available to divorcing couples.

It is nonadversarial. Divorce mediation assumes that divorcing couples can and do share the same goal: reaching a fair and equitable settlement of all divorce-related issues while respecting individual needs, providing future security, and maintaining self-respect and dignity. Experience shows that when given an opportunity, most couples in mediation are able to trust each other; even in the presence of intense pain, they make decisions that express their concern for each other.

The basic assumption in a traditional divorce is that the other party will act in his or her self-interest at all times. Therefore, a great deal of time and energy is spent anticipating and blocking the other party's actions, which are assumed to be self-motivated. The divorce mediator is unique in helping couples keep away from adversarial thinking.

Mediation assumes that most divorcing couples are able to consider the needs and interests of others. I have found that, most of the time, this assumption proves to be true.

It focuses on values, not positions. Despite the intensity of their anger and pain, couples choose divorce mediation because they want to stay focused on agreement and be held accountable to a neutral third party for their behavior. One man put it this way:

> We both wanted to avoid a big fight. We have two children we love dearly. We wanted to be fair with each other. And we wanted to remain friends. We had heard too many horror stories about people going through divorce who ended up hating each other and fighting over their kids. We didn't want that.

The mediator does not represent the specific interest of either spouse. Rather, the mediator encourages caring, respect, compromise, and agreement—values desperately needed during any divorce transition.

It acknowledges and supports feelings. The neutral acknowledgment of deeply felt feelings is perhaps the most important of mediation's unique characteristics. But while feelings are acknowledged and sometimes explored, the mediator guides their expression in ways that enhance and encourage understanding, support, and ultimately agreement. A mediator skilled in dealing with the emotional issues of divorce can explain the nature of divorce to couples and give them guidance about dealing safely with the feelings they have about the divorce. A mediator skilled in dealing with the spiritual issues of divorce can help a divorcing couple to draw on deeply held spiritual values and preserve the dignity of each party, acknowledging God's presence in their lives in spite of the deep void they may feel.

What if One Wants a Divorce and the Other Doesn't?

Mediation cannot reform individuals, alter personalities, or create love and trust where none exists. The methods and processes of mediation, however, permit the fullest possible expression of the values of respect, caring, and compassion. Mediation is able to access these emotions because of its singular approach to conflict and differences.

For mediation to be successful, both spouses must eventually participate fully, although they may not begin that way. Many couples begin mediation with deeply entrenched, mutually exclusive positions but leave with agreements that represent compromise, respect, and caring. Mediated agreements tend to be more generous than the law requires—the natural consequence of an other-oriented negotiation rather than the adversarial I-focused approach. Divorcing couples often discover that getting what they want does not necessarily mean preventing the other person from finding satisfaction too.

Maintaining decision-making power. Without judging the rightness or wrongness of individual positions, the mediator can guide couples in reaching their own decisions. Each spouse participates in reaching the decision and in so doing brings to that process his or her own sense of fairness.

Mediation Is Not Marriage Counseling

Allen and Beth came to mediation when they first started talking about divorce. It quickly became clear that they were undecided about divorce, so I suggested they seek marriage counseling, which eventually led to marital and family therapy. After two years of counseling, they are again considering whether to divorce, but doing so with a deeper sense of self and other.

Marital or individual therapy tries to define psychological barriers to individual or marital happiness and to eliminate barriers through exploration of their psychological roots. The counseling or therapy is directed at enhancing the individual's, couple's, or family's emotional and psychological health.

Although certain skills and techniques used in counseling may be used in mediation, the purpose of mediation is neither to save or reconcile a marriage nor to improve the well-being of the individuals or the marriage relationship. However, mediation frequently leads to improved communication and reduced conflict. In some instances, mediation actually leads to reconciliation. In such cases, the mediator should refer the couple immediately to marital or couple counseling.

Mediation Is Not Arbitration

Do not confuse mediation with its close cousin, arbitration. In mediation, spouses themselves retain complete decision-making power and responsibility. Arbitration, on the other hand, puts the decision-making power into the hands of a neutral third party who renders either a binding or nonbinding decision.

In some cases, a couple in mediation may agree on all but one or two issues. The mediator saves the couple time and money by suggesting arbitration rather than litigating the issues before a judge. If the couple elects arbitration, they can pick one or several arbitrators from a list of recommended specialists and then submit the unresolved issues to arbitration.

Through mediation, Amy and Steve (whom you met in chapter 2) agreed on child custody, division of property, health insurance, and education costs for their children, but they were unable to agree on the length and amount of child and spousal support. Their situation was complicated by the recent loss of both their jobs, the emotional trauma resulting from the divorce, and their long history of misunderstanding each other's motives.

When emotional and financial fears paralyzed their decision-making abilities, Amy and Steve agreed to submit the issues of spousal and child support to arbitration and to accept the arbitrated decision. They picked two arbitrators from a list of qualified professionals. The arbitrators examined the facts, then rendered binding decisions.

The mediator should talk about the process as it unfolds, particularly when the couple is at an impasse or when a problem arises, and call attention to progress as it is achieved. At times it is difficult for the couple to see their progress; the mediator can reflect on the progress as a neutral observer, pointing out when they move from disagreement to agreement.

Conclusion

Perhaps the single most important factor in determining the success of mediation is getting the process started as early as possible. Many couples wait until the anger and hostility levels are so high that they severely inhibit communication.

Remember: Mediation is only as successful as the intent of the couple to make it work. The mediator, no matter how skilled at resolving differences, cannot make people agree when they are intent on fighting, or create respect and compassion where hatred and anger prevail. For this reason, mediation does not work for all couples. For those who are eager to preserve their personal dignity, express respect for each other, and lessen the pain of divorce, mediation is a viable alternative.

Chapter 5

What About the Children?

Child custody and child support are two of the most difficult areas to mediate. When it works, the children are the clear winners. When child-related issues rage on unresolved, the children pay an enormous price for their parents' war.

During child custody and child support disputes, issues loom that were never resolved during the marriage, issues such as lifestyle differences, discipline, grooming, nutrition, and the primacy of the mother's or father's role. In some instances, the marital conflict continues beyond the final divorce decree as parents battle over the children. Often, the care and custody of the children are used as leverage in negotiations about the amount of spousal or child support to be paid.

Wallace and Linda

When Wallace and Linda came to mediation, their only disagreement was the custody of their three children. They had already agreed on the division of property and support payments. Since separating from Linda, Wallace had developed an intimate relationship with another woman, who was now living in his apartment. Linda, on the other hand, was certain she would not remarry, and she felt Wallace's lifestyle was an inappropriate model for the children.

Wallace wanted as much time with the children as possible. Linda felt Wallace's only motivation was to reduce the amount he had to pay her for child support. During the marriage, Linda had stayed at home with the children while Wallace had been the primary income earner. Linda was not about to give up the role of primary parent and allow Wallace to suddenly become an equal parent. "Where were you all those years when I was home with the kids?" Linda demanded.

Wallace responded, "And where were you when I was out earning the money to keep us all alive?" Wallace implied that Linda should have been earning money during the marriage and should certainly be doing so now.

The goal of child custody mediation is to transform connections among the parents and children so that the children have healthy and happy relationships with both parents despite the fact that the parents lead separate lives. How a parent interacts with the children will directly impact not only the children but the other parent as well.

Why Mediate Child-Related Matters?

Extensive research on children of divorce has produced this clear conclusion: High-level conflict between divorcing parents negatively impacts the children; children of divorcing parents who have learned to manage conflict do far better in later life (Wallerstein and Blakeslee 1987).

Dr. Edward Beal of Georgetown University Medical School recently conducted a study of three hundred divorcing families, following them for twenty years beginning at the time of the divorce. Beal compared his findings to a control group of intact families. He found that the children of highly conflicted parents experienced more dating anxiety during adolescence and young adulthood than children of intact families. Later in life, the girls of highly conflicted divorced parents had a 64 percent higher divorce rate than the girls of intact families, and the boys had a 33 percent higher divorce rate than their counterparts (Gannett News Service, 14 May 1991).

Any approach that can reduce the level of conflict, animosity, and hostility provides the children of divorce a greater

chance of developing successful and healthy relationships
in later life.

Court-Ordered Custody Mediation

Many states require mediation in cases involving a child-
related dispute. In their state, Linda and Wallace would
have been ordered into mediation had they not voluntarily
sought private mediation for resolving all their issues, including those related to the children.

It is important that the divorcing couple talk with several
different mediators to select the one most appropriate for
them. Things to consider in making this selection are the
needs of the children, accessibility and time availability of
the mediator, and the mediator's apparent knowledge,
skill, and experience in guiding decisions. Wallace and
Linda wished to address all the issues of their divorce in
mediation and not be limited to only those relating to the
children, so they looked for a mediator that was not limited
in expertise. For Wallace and Linda, it was clear that their
child custody conflict was directly related to the way in
which each thought of the other's position on child support
and other financial issues.

Child custody mediation usually brings to the surface such
intense emotions as fear, insecurity, abandonment anxiety,
and anger. These emotions surface most easily during child
custody mediation, thus making the discussions highly
volatile. Resolving such feelings and reaching workable
agreements often requires dealing with financial and property issues in conjunction with child-related issues, making resolution complex and difficult.

Custody Laws

It is essential that the divorcing couple know and understand the law pertaining to child custody. The representa-

tive or advising attorney or the divorce mediator will, most usually, be an informed source. In most states, self-help aids describing child custody and child support laws are available in bookstores or local libraries. Becoming informed through one's own research is an excellent way to prepare for mediation.

Over the years, the issue of child custody has been divided into legal and physical custody. This division allows couples to separate child-related matters into natural and manageable categories.

Legal and Physical Custody

Legal custody is the right, duty and obligation to participate in decisions affecting the child's health, education, or welfare. Generally speaking, this means that Dad is still Dad and Mom is still Mom.

Jill and Fred discussed which form of legal custody (joint or sole—see below) best fit their wishes and desires. They decided that joint legal custody would mean that they would decide together where the children would attend school, whether the kids would go to summer camp, and whether and what type of medical attention would be required in a particular instance. They agreed to discuss overarching issues that affect the children and agree on the payment of any associated costs.

Physical custody, on the other hand, has to do with daily care and management of the children. Most child custody disputes focus on the extent to which the parents are involved with the children on a daily basis.

Joint or Sole Custody

Legal and physical custody can be either joint or sole. Joint custody means that custody is shared by the parents. Sole custody means that one or the other parent retains all the decision-making power for the child and that the other parent may not participate in those decisions at all.

Many divorcing couples assume that joint physical custody means a fifty-fifty time share of the children. This is not the case. If the couple decides on joint physical custody, then they are free to arrange parenting that best fits the care and scheduling they desire for their children. Victoria and Rod decided on joint legal and physical custody, but the children stayed with Victoria all week long and went to Rod's house only on the weekends. Renee and Arthur chose joint legal and physical custody, but the children were with Arthur three nights a week and with Renee four nights.

Family law courts generally interpret joint custody as an agreement between the parents to take responsibility for their children. The courts give the parents the freedom to make arrangements that are best for the parents and the children. In granting joint custody it is as if the court has declared that it will not interfere in the parenting of the children and will only become involved in custody or parenting issues at the request of one of the spouses or at the initiative of the state authorities.

If the couple decides on one parent's having sole physical custody, the final judgment of the court will contain specified visitation rights for the noncustodial parent. The court will enforce the visitation rights in the event of a disagreement.

Sam and Beverly

When Sam and Beverly first came to mediation, Beverly insisted on sole physical custody of their child, Rachel. Sam wanted more time with Rachel, but Beverly was convinced that at Rachel's age it was better for Rachel to be with her mother. At the time, Rachel was spending two or three days a week with Sam but in the summer might spend more time with him. Beverly did not want Rachel to spend time during the week with Sam during the school year, but she was willing to look at the possibility of increasing Sam's time with Rachel during the summer.

After Sam and Beverly discussed the meaning of legal and physical, sole and joint custody, Beverly began to see that joint legal and physical custody better represented their present arrangements and more accurately described what she and Sam hoped the arrangements would be like in the future. We discovered that Beverly's insistence on sole physical custody had a great deal to do with the anger she felt toward Sam about the divorce. As Beverly learned to express her anger more freely, she became less insistent on sole physical custody and more open to the idea of joint custody. Sam and Beverly ended that session agreeing to joint custody. Rachel's primary home would be Beverly's house. They recognized that each was a good parent to Rachel and a supportive parenting partner for the other.

Mediation sessions like Béverly and Sam's are the most gratifying. Within a brief time Sam and Beverly experienced how open and honest discussion and the sharing of feelings clears the air and brings a sense of reconciliation and connection.

Child Support

Standardized child support guidelines are available to divorcing couples in many states. These guidelines are usually based on three factors: the husband's net income, the wife's net income, and the amount of time the children spend with each parent. These guidelines are available through each county court or the county law library and have been put into computer programs available to attorneys, mediators, and others.

The guidelines do not, however, eliminate disputes over child and spousal support, nor do they diminish the value of mediation. In practice, the data used to calculate the guidelines is subject to a wide range of interpretation and can vary significantly from one computation to another. One attorney recently described to me a court appearance on the issue of spousal and child support. He and the opposing attorney had prepared their presentations using the computerized support guidelines; they both believed that they had been completely objective. Their calculations, however, differed by more than three thousand dollars a month.

For this reason, the guidelines are best used simply as directional tools to help the couple begin discussing child and spousal support. Ultimately, the couple's decision should be based not only on the guidelines but also on what is needed, how much income is available, and in what ways the children can best be supported. In most divorce cases, financial needs increase because the spouses must support two households instead of one, yet the income pie remains the same.

Common Issues
in Child Custody Mediation

The two issues that most commonly come up during child custody mediation are the shifting roles of parents and differences in lifestyle.

Shifting Parental Roles

A frequent complaint, particularly of divorcing mothers, is that the heretofore absent parent, often the father, now wants to be an active and participating parent. This stirs up great resentment in the care-giving parent, who suddenly finds this role threatened.

In most of these cases the perception of the facts is accurate. Many parents, particularly fathers, assumed the role of primary income earner and relied on the homemaking and parenting skills of the spouse to raise the children and manage the home. In many instances, these roles were assumed without discussion; they simply evolved from traditional social roles.

When a divorce or separation happens, the roles of both parents are upset. Many times the primary income earner wants the formerly dependent spouse to become employed in order to reduce the financial stress of spousal and child support. The absent parent begins to realize that being a single parent means developing a relationship with the children independent of the homemaker spouse. These changes in roles often create great stress and result in a realignment of values and roles.

Elaine and Randy

When Elaine and Randy divorced, they fell into immediate conflict over their parental roles. Since the children were only four and six years old, Elaine felt they still needed to be with their mother. She felt it was her duty to continue being the primary parent, as she had been since the children were born. Randy, a full-time employed professional, felt that he should have the children an equal amount of time— even if it meant child care would be necessary—thereby freeing Elaine to pursue a career.

It was difficult for Elaine to understand Randy's new desire to be an active parent. Randy and Elaine wrestled with these issues in mediation until they were able to agree upon a workable solution. Elaine would have the children most of the time throughout the week. A couple of nights during the week, they would stay with Randy. He would pick them up from school and take them to school the next morning. Elaine found a part-time job that allowed her the flexibility necessary to be the primary parent. Randy and Elaine agreed that they would continue this arrangement until the children were older and that they would review the situation every year.

Lifestyle Differences

Differences in the parents' lifestyles following separation is a common problem frequently dealt with in mediation. These lifestyle changes often erupt into child custody disputes when one parent wishes to prevent the children from being exposed to the lifestyle of the other.

Peter and Sylvia, Kathy and Russ

When Peter and Sylvia separated, Sylvia not only continued to be active in their church but increased her involvement. Peter, on the other hand, stopped going to church at all and started to drink much more than he had before. In addition, he started dating right away and would often bring his dates to his apartment.

When Sylvia found out about Peter's behavior, she hit the roof. Under no circumstances, according to her, would the children be permitted at Peter's apartment either when he was drinking or when Peter's girlfriends were there. Peter did not take kindly to what he perceived as Sylvia's interference. He believed that what he did was his own business.

The problem was that they were both right. As a divorced person, Peter was free to live his life as he chose. Sylvia, on the other hand, was appropriately concerned about the children and what they were exposed to.

For Kathy and Russ, the issue was the type of movies Russ either brought home for the kids to watch or took them to see at the cinema. Kathy did not feel the children should see movies with explicit sex or violence, while Russ felt there was nothing wrong with the children seeing movies where sex, fighting, and shooting were a part of the story.

In such cases, there is little that can be done to stop a parent from living as they choose. Unless there is evidence of child abuse or molestation, the courts are reluctant to take away parental rights. Thus, while one parent may receive sole physical custody of the children, the other parent will be granted visitation rights. The behavior or lifestyle of the visiting parent can not be controlled or limited by the courts.

The best approach to solving lifestyle differences, painful and difficult as it will be, is for the parents to remain in communication. When parents are able to talk with each other, they can try to influence the other's decisions with gentle persuasion and education. As soon as parents cease to communicate, the influence one parent can play in the life of the other is reduced significantly.

Peter and Sylvia were able to work out an agreement. Peter agreed to curtail his drinking around the kids and never drive with the children in the car if he drank any alcohol. Furthermore, Peter and Sylvia agreed that they would not expose the children to girlfriends or boyfriends unless they had been seeing that person for a long time and a serious relationship had developed.

Kathy and Russ were unable to resolve their differences. Eventually, they each retained lawyers and had their differences settled in court. Because of their conflicts, Kathy was awarded sole physical custody, but Russ was granted absolute visitation rights every weekend. Kathy could do nothing about the movies Russ showed the kids except talk with the children when they came back to her care.

The Children Come First

While many people give lip service to the idea of putting the needs of the children first, a surprisingly large number of couples are unable to do so. They often withhold the children from the other parent, fight for control of the children's daily habits, or argue that the other parent is unfit for parenting because he or she has a new dating partner or spouse.

They excuse this behavior by saying it is for the children's sake. The opposite is usually closer to the truth. The children are the pawns in the marriage conflict, used by parents to wound each other. This form of indirect conflict often indicates that mediation will not be successful.

When parents are truly able to put the interests of the children first, successful mediation is virtually assured. Roger and Ann are a perfect example.

Roger and Ann

In spite of deeply held anger toward each other and resentment over events during the marriage, Roger and Ann agreed to consult with a child psychologist for guidance on how best to deal with Jimmy, their seven-year-old son. They watched carefully for signs of depression or maladjustment in school, spent time with him separately to assure him of their continuing involvement as parents, and made sure he got time with both Roger's and Ann's family. When Ann announced that she had decided to move to another part of the state, they discussed at length the various options for Jimmy's care. Finally, after careful evaluation, they decided to try an approach that allowed them both to continue to be involved in Jimmy's life. They agreed that if Jimmy showed any signs of not adjusting to Ann's new home, she would move back to town.

Aware of their own biases and possibly impaired decision-making abilities, Roger and Ann relied on the mediator and the child psychologist to help them stay focused on Jimmy. The willingness to submit their individual desires to whatever would best serve Jimmy and his development took great courage. Their genuine desire to do this was an important clue that their mediation would succeed.

Bob and Tamera

In contrast, Bob and Tamera's inability to separate their own wants from their children's needs resulted in a three-year battle for child custody that was resolved only through the courts. Tamera was unable to contain her anger toward Bob; Bob used the children to continue his rigid and controlling behavior. They fought over anything and everything having to do with the children. Tamera thought Bob was too easy with the kids and not concerned enough with their safety. Bob thought Tamera was too protective of the children, forbidding them to enjoy or experience childhood. They fought over what clothes the children wore, what schools they should attend, and what the other parent should or should not do while the children were present. Their custody conflicts had taken them to four different psychologists, three different mediators, and, eventually, several different lawyers. Their inability to put the children's needs before their own was a sure sign of their inability to mediate.

Conclusion

Resolving child-related issues is one of the most beneficial results of mediation. As noted above, in many states, the value of mediation is so clearly recognized that it is required by the courts for all child custody issues. Although the parents gain a great deal by mediating child-related issues, the real winners are the children. They see the parents resolving issues openly and with respect for each other, and they see communication continue beyond mediation.

Studies show that children would prefer their parents to stay married even if they are not happy together (Sapoznek 1983). When children of divorcing parents see their mother and father working out differences in constructive ways, the children gain a clear sense that both parents will remain active in their lives. The children also gain confidence from knowing that their parents love them enough to maintain communication and to find solutions that work for everyone.

There is no message more important for the children to receive than this: Their mother and father love them and will not let anything get in the way of that relationship.

Chapter 6

What Happens if . . . ?

Human nature being what it is, we frequently imagine the worst possible scenarios for any new idea. The "But what happens if . . . ?" question leads to a variety of other important questions. What happens if we don't reach agreement? What happens if we reach agreement on all but one or two issues? Do we then have to go to court? What happens if I find that he has taken money from our accounts? What happens if she won't let me see the kids?

There Are Always Other Options to Mediation

Couples entering mediation are often concerned about losing leverage in negotiation. They are concerned that once mediation begins, they lose the right to a litigated, adversarial approach. In fact, however, the parties may decide to end the mediation at any time. Couples in voluntary mediation never lose the option of switching to another approach.

From Mediation to Litigation

Actually, switching from mediation to a litigated process is easy and quick. If the mediating spouses have already retained legal counsel, they can simply tell their attorneys that mediation failed. The attorneys will pick up the negotiation process with each other. If the mediating spouses have not yet retained attorneys and have not filed any court papers themselves, they may simply hire attorneys. If the couple started the divorce process by filing the initial court documents themselves, they can hire attorneys who will then complete and file a simple one-page form titled "Substitution of Attorney." The new attorneys immediately become the attorneys of record.

Lauren and Mason

Lauren and Mason began their divorce using mediation. They decided to use a paralegal to file, hoping to keep the cost to a minimum and avoid a battle. Mason, an attorney himself, was well aware of the pitfalls of the adversarial approach. They each acted as their own legal representatives *In Pro Per*. Mason and Lauren met regularly for many months, discussing the market values of their two homes, community investments, and Mason's pension benefits. They fought a great deal about child custody and support.

Although Mason and Lauren reached agreement on nearly all issues, they were unable to come to final agreement and ultimately terminated the mediation. Lauren borrowed money from a relative and hired a lawyer, who immediately became her representative. Mason retained his own counsel. Through their respective legal counsel they eventually concluded their divorce.

From Litigation to Mediation

Switching from litigation to mediation should be as easy as switching from mediation to litigation. It is not always. Theoretically, the couple electing to mediate after having begun an adversarial process need only tell their legal representatives that they are meeting in mediation, where they hope an agreement will be reached. Many attorneys are very supportive of mediation and will encourage mediation where possible. Other attorneys are hostile toward mediation and will discourage couples from using it. In either case, it is the couple's or individual's decision whether or not to use mediation. They can discuss the decision with their representative attorney.

Alternative Dispute Resolution

Between entirely self-directed mediation—during which the parties act as their own representatives and the divorce is handled by mail—and full-blown litigation, there are a number of very reasonable alternatives for people who are unable to resolve one or more issues. These alternatives are referred to in the legal profession as Alternative Dispute Resolution, or ADR.

The first form of ADR is mediation, the subject of this book. Couples who are representing themselves *In Pro Per* or who are represented by attorneys can use mediation. Resistance to mediation is rapidly diminishing among the legal profession. Increasing numbers of attorneys are seeking specialized training in mediation, and mediation is receiving attention at the annual meetings of the American Bar Association. James Melamed, executive director of the Academy of Family Mediators, calls this change of roles and professional consciousness a shift of historic proportions. He goes on to say that "Bar Associations and legislatures across America are now recognizing the unlimited potential of mediation to constructively resolve conflict" (Melamed 1989, 14). This is a sign that mediation will be used increasingly in the years ahead.

Arbitration

A second option is arbitration, a close cousin to mediation. A critical distinction between the two is that in arbitration, the decision-making power is given over to a neutral third party who renders a binding or nonbinding decision. In mediation, the decision-making power remains with the couple.

In the discussion in chapter 4 about mediation and arbitration, I described Amy and Steve's experience with arbitration. Using mediation, they had agreed on all issues but those of spousal and child support. Amy felt the support should be based on what Steve made at the time of separation. Steve, who had lost his job after separating, wanted to base support on his present income level, although he was willing to pay more even if it meant drawing from his separate funds to do so. Amy and Steve consulted separate attorneys and believed they were right in their positions. At the suggestion of the mediator, they agreed to submit these issues to arbitration.

Amy and Steve picked two arbitrators from a list of qualified family law attorneys, child psychologists, and retired judges. The mediator prepared a written statement of the history of the mediation, identifying the remaining issues of spousal and child support. Amy and Steve prepared statements from their own perspectives, including as many facts and details as they felt appropriate.

They decided not to be represented by attorneys in the arbitration. They had acted as their own representatives throughout the mediation process and, in the interest of containing costs, elected to continue into arbitration without legal representatives.

After receiving the written statements, the arbitrators set a hearing time. They spoke with Steve and Amy separately, giving the spouses an opportunity to discuss their perspectives on the issues. Several weeks later, the arbitrators rendered their decision, which was then submitted to the court for approval. Amy and Steve did not have to appear in court.

By agreement between Amy and Steve, the arbitrators' decision was binding. Had they preferred, the decision could have been nonbinding and advisory only. In that case, the decision would have been used as a barometer from which they would mediate an agreement.

Amy and Steve's arbitration was much faster and far less costly than the traditional adversarial approach. What's more, they were able to preserve the progress they had made in mediation and use arbitration to resolve specific issues. Had they opted to end mediation when they were unable to come to agreement on spousal and child support, they might have had to start over again, with each issue becoming part of the adversarial process.

Private Judicial Review

Another alternative to the traditional litigation process is private judicial review. Couples can hire on an hourly basis an experienced judge, retired or semiretired, to render decisions. These judges act outside the established court structures. They may handle the judicial review as they would an arbitration, or they may conduct a hearing much like that which would occur in the court room. The private judicial review is becoming increasingly popular, particularly for complicated divorces. Couples interested in this alternative can contract one of the agencies listed in the Appendix for a referral.

The benefits of private judicial review are cost and speed. A private judicial review costs significantly less than a litigated divorce and can occur much more quickly. When speed is essential, consider a private judicial review.

An Unusual Example

Although not a divorce case, the following description of a custody dispute is a good example of arbitration in conjunction with family mediation.

Sally gave birth to Melinda while still in high school. After abandoning Melinda after a wild party, Sally was forced to give up custody. Sally's parents, not wanting their grandchild to be placed in a foster home, petitioned the court and were made legal guardians of Melinda. They raised her the first five years of her life.

During that time, Sally began to turn her life around. She showed increasing responsibility for Melinda's care and eventually asked her parents to transfer custody back to her. Her parents would have been delighted to do so were it not for her becoming a Jehovah's Witness. They understood that Jehovah's Witnesses oppose celebrations and go so far as to encourage disassociation with non-Witnesses, even family members who do not share their belief. Sally's parents were attached to their granddaughter. They felt they could not give Sally guardianship of Melinda knowing that they might be prevented from ever seeing Melinda again.

Sally and her parents agreed to mediate their differences with my assistance, but they eventually reached an impasse. Together they considered their alternatives and selected arbitration. They selected a pediatrician, a social worker, and a family counselor as their arbitrators from a list of experts.

The arbitrators met together and then met with Sally, her parents, and five-year-old Melinda. The arbitrators then recommended that guardianship be transferred back to Sally, the natural mother, and that all four enter individual counseling and family counseling.

Sally and her parents followed the arbitrators' recommendations in every detail. At first, the relationship between Sally and her parents was strained, but as they put into effect the arbitrators' recommendations they were able to work through their conflicts, and they came to love and respect each other in new ways. Four years later I received a call from Sally inviting me to her college graduation. She, her parents, and Melinda were all doing fine. Her parents see Melinda regularly, and Sally often spends time with them at their home. By this time, Sally had pulled away from the Jehovah's Witnesses. The family had been saved from a great deal of pain.

Conclusion

There is no guarantee that mediation will result in agreement and resolve all conflict. Mediation simply provides a decision-making approach that emphasizes cooperation and guides the parties away from an adversarial stance. If the mediation is unsuccessful, the couple can quickly and easily implement an adversarial approach, substitute attorneys as their representatives, and have the issues resolved in court. Or they can choose arbitration or private judicial review.

Couples who begin divorce using mediation usually experience improved communication and enhanced decision-making. If another approach is required later in the process, the mediation experience often makes the alternative easier and simpler.

Chapter 7

What Does the Spirit Have to Do with Mediation?

Many Christians see marriage and the relationship it signifies as a reflection of the intimate relationship the human being has with God and God's presence through the Holy Spirit. The union of marriage is often equated with the union of Christ with the church, a relationship of oneness and completeness. But what happens when that union dissolves into unbearable pain and suffering? Is the divorcing couple's relationship with God also broken and dissolved?

Of course, the answer to this question is a resounding no. Paul assures us of this in Romans 8:38–39 when he says that nothing can separate us from the love of God as that love is experienced in the life, death, and resurrection of Jesus the Christ. In spite of our faith in God's everlasting love, many divorcing couples experience condemnation—both internally and by the community of faith. This condemnation often leads to a downward spiritual spiral, an unfortunate consequence of applying the metaphor of marriage to the spiritual relationship we, as people of faith, have with God.

Aware of this spiritual tug-of-war, the divorce mediator may be one of the few people not only to lead divorcing couples toward peaceful resolution of differences and conflict but also to function in ways that reassure couples of the continuing love, forgiveness, and grace of God. Biblical principles of shalom, reconciliation, and justice—evidence of the Spirit—are more apparent and realizable in and through a mediated approach to divorce than in an approach based on competing interests, adversarial reasoning, and heightened suspicion.

An often thought—but unspoken—question about mediation is, "Why would I want to mediate?" The answer to this question has everything to do with the role mediation can have in assuring and affirming the presence of the Holy Spirit in the lives of the divorcing couple and family.

Carol and Murray

Carol and Murray, both active members of their church, had been married only a few years and had one child, Alyson. Murray came from a wealthy family; Carol did not. When unhappiness in the relationship drove them apart, Carol filed for divorce through her attorney. Murray responded through his attorney. They began to battle over who controlled the family residence, how to distribute marital property, and who owed money to whom.

Months later, after each had spent thousands of dollars in legal fees without even a hint of agreement, Carol and Murray sought mediation at the recommendation of their pastor. For three meetings, the mediator showed them that their pain need not become negative judgment about the other. The mediator often rephrased their negative and hurtful comments in ways that highlighted and addressed the emotions behind the statement rather than the judgment the statement carried. Many times the mediator explained that the intention behind a question or statement was to be helpful, but it had been filtered through the anger and pain of the other, so it was understood as critical or abusive.

Over time Carol and Murray began to see their respect for each other emerge from the ruins of their decision to divorce and began to experience a coming together through agreement and understanding. Eventually, Carol and Murray were able to speak about their hopes for each other following divorce and to recognize that God loved and cared for each of them and their child in, through, and even in spite of their divorce.

The Optimal Environment for Mediation

The optimal environment for mediation is one of mutual trust and respect. Agreement becomes easier when the divorcing couple feels that each is being honest and trustworthy, that both are striving for a fair and equitable settlement. Creating such an environment is often difficult, because divorce, almost by definition, creates contrary feelings among the divorcing spouses. Creating an open and accepting environment, however, can be one of the goals of mediation.

To counter the natural tendencies of divorce to encourage mistrust and fear, the mediator works to see that love, forgiveness, and reconciliation are a part of the divorce process. This approach stands in contrast to most approaches to this transition and the necessity of reaching agreement, emphasizing the benefits to each spouse of a cooperative, mediated approach and the spiritual benefits that would result from a less hostile divorce.

Leaving Judgment to God

A pastoral colleague of mine has on his study wall a framed quote by Robert Davies which sums up how God's Spirit works in mediation. It reads, "Moral judgments belong to God, and it is part of the divine mercy that we do not have to undertake that heavy part of God's work, even when the judgment concerns ourselves." Not only are others free from judgment in mediation, but so are we.

When people of faith assume that others are at heart generous, caring, and compassionate, they are living Jesus' teaching to look for the log in one's own eye before pointing out the speck in another's. Christians find it possible to believe

God's Spirit is present in mediation when the spouses, with
the help of the mediator if necessary, leave judgment of each
other behind, taking advantage of the fresh opportunity to
show understanding and support in reaching agreement.

Denise and Robert

Denise and Robert had been married for about eight years.
They were devout Christians and active in their church.
Robert, however, had several psychological problems that
stemmed from childhood abuse by an alcoholic father. The
stress in the relationship drove Denise to separate from
Robert.

Denise filed for legal separation. She explained to Robert
that although she was not seeking an end to the relationship, she had to file for legal separation in order to receive
county support for herself and their child. She invited
Robert to join her in counseling, something Denise and
Robert's pastor urged for them both. Robert was adamantly
opposed and refused to consider counseling.

When Denise filed for legal separation, it so angered Robert
that he counter-filed for divorce. They began to fight over
custody of their son. Under the court rules of the state in
which they lived, they were required to go to mediation on
child-related matters. After several sessions of court-
sponsored mediation, they were still in conflict about who
would get physical custody and about the rights each would
have as legal custodian of their child.

Denise heard about private mediation and suggested it to
Robert. Robert, initially hesitant, agreed only after meeting
a mediator by chance (or was it the leading of the Spirit?) at
a local business meeting.

The mediation session began with a review of the couple's
history. The mediator listened to their story, interpreting
out loud, without judgment, the feelings that had motivated each action or event. Slowly, the defensive walls

crumbled; in their place emerged a true desire on both sides to work toward reconciliation. They left that mediation session with a fresh new look at their parenting goals and with the hope of sharing the parenting of their child jointly.

Several months later Denise sent the mediator a thank-you card. Since meeting in mediation, she and Robert had gotten together for supper and spoken many times without fighting. They were now talking about how they might get back together. Denise went on to write that Robert, who had absolutely refused counseling, saying he "would die first," had agreed to begin couple counseling. One sentence in her note was particularly poignant: "In my life I have seen the Lord work *one* large miracle—this is the *second*—and it's still hard to believe."

In mediation, Denise and Robert experienced a nonjudgmental environment where they were able to examine the issues in conflict between them. They were not condemned for their actions; rather, they gained a sense of understanding and forgiveness for all that had transpired. They were allowed to tell their story from their own perspective. Their motivations and interests were interpreted in a respectful, nonjudgmental way. They walked in each other's shoes for the first time, hearing the emotions behind each action. In this way the door of forgiveness and understanding was opened. In one sense they experienced a moment of grace, a transcendent moment where "Judge not, that ye be not judged" (Matt. 7:1, KJV) was more than just words on a page.

Denise and Robert are extremely rare in that their experience of mediation led to the reconciliation of their relationship. Such reconciliations should not be expected; nor should mediation be used for the purpose of reconciling.

Love One Another

A pastoral colleague once described his meeting with a woman who was having post-divorce complications with her former husband. The issues centered on his failure to pay spousal and child support and conflicts over the visitation schedule. The pastor gave her an assignment to pray for her former husband every day for one week in fulfillment of their marriage vows which, he interpreted for her, meant to love her husband until death. He explained to her that these vows did not say live with him, share the same bed with him, or be in an oppressive relationship with him, but to love him.

That week she faithfully fulfilled the assignment. She returned to see the pastor the following week with joy in her eyes and a smile on her face and in her heart. "It works! It really works!" she exclaimed. She went on to describe how she felt less hostile toward her former husband and how in turn he talked openly and without anger about the problems they had to resolve.

The pastor had understood Jesus' ethical imperative to love your enemies as yourself and realized that there was a reward for such love that was, at times, beyond understanding. More important, he shared that message with the divorced woman in a way that permitted her to experience the Savior he knew and loved.

Mediation permits couples to build on a solid foundation of respect and understanding rather than on the assumption that they must defend against each other's hurtful tendencies. They begin with the assumption that they can work together to reach agreements that are mutually acceptable and supportive.

Defending Against Hate; Seeking Forgiveness

If evil has a stronghold, it is in the hate that many divorcing spouses hold for each other. This fortress is nearly impenetrable, and it will accept self-destruction before capitulation. The guards of the fortress of hate are most often pain, fear, and rejection. Mediation may shift the focus of thoughts and actions away from assaulting the fortress to focusing on forgiveness, understanding, and compassion.

In his book, *Forgive and Forget: Healing the Hurts We Don't Deserve,* Lewis Smedes says that forgiveness is not just forgetting, not just excusing, not just smothering conflict, not just accepting, and not just tolerating. Rather, forgiveness is letting go of the painful past. It is the miraculous release of malice from the spirit to experience the love that restores broken relationships.

Smedes reminds his readers that the past cannot be erased, but the pain from the past can be healed. This is the reason that mediation, while acknowledging the past, withholds judgment of past actions and begins in the present. Mediation offers a fresh new beginning in which to resolve differences.

Sometimes I ask couples at the outset of mediation if the other spouse has been hurtful. Because of the nature of divorce, the answer is usually yes. Then I ask if they would like to stop hurting each other. Sometimes it is actually necessary to have each say to the other, "I would like to stop hurting you."

At the moment that each realizes that the past is forgiven, the couple can begin to treat each other in a new and kinder way, approaching issues with the intent of helping each other through the process. The wish they exchange is, in many instances, the first kind and encouraging message they have shared in weeks, months, even years. The moment is often a breakthrough of feelings and emotions.

Reconciliation of the Suffering

Besides seeking justice and fairness in the marital agreement, pastoral mediation often leads to a form of reconciliation between the partners and children of a dissolving marriage. I call it a form of reconciliation because it helps bring together people who may be alienated from each other by irreconcilable differences and from God by feelings of guilt, failure, and loneliness. The pastoral mediator de-mythologizes the divorce process and promotes the re-demptive possibilities for both the individual and the family. John B. Cobb calls this form of pastoral intervention the act of being a "midwife of God's grace" (Cobb 1977, 52).

Perhaps the most compelling biblical reference to reconcil-iation is found in Colossians 1:15–20. Here Paul formulates an understanding of Christ as the complete reconciler, putting into order all things visible and invisible, earthly or heavenly. Paul sees Christ holding all things together in himself through the fullness of God.

This idea provides perhaps the truest understanding of reconciliation through mediation. Through Jesus Christ and the presence of the Holy Spirit, the pastoral mediator assists the divorcing couple in looking with hope toward what lies beyond the divorce while gently and carefully bringing the conflicted parties to agreement.

In a sense, the pastoral mediator dignifies the death of the marriage and nurtures the new life that begins to grow during the mediation process. This is why the question I often ask couples at the beginning of the first session—"Is this mar-riage over?"—is so poignant. It confronts the mediating cou-ple with the reality of their choice to divorce, permits us to acknowledge the death of the marriage, and allows them to begin preparing for life beyond its confining walls.

At the same time, the role of the pastoral mediator is to understand the need for grief and the suffering inherent in the divorce process while hinting at the possibilities that lie ahead. Pierre Teilhard de Chardin expresses this under-standing of suffering in this way:

> What a vast ocean of human suffering spread over the entire earth at every moment! Of what is this mass formed? Of blackness, gaps and rejections? No, let me repeat, of poten-tial energy. In suffering the world's upward force is cancelled in a very intense form. The whole question is how

to liberate it and give it a consciousness of its significance and potentialities. (Teilhard de Chardin 1974, 102)

When the mediator acknowledges and celebrates the options available as part of the negotiation process, suffering is converted into creative hope, invariably turning barriers into building blocks, problems into challenges, and options into solutions.

Justice and Fairness

For many couples, respecting each other in the midst of divorce is difficult or even impossible. Therefore, rather than seek to achieve reconciliation with your divorcing partner, it is more appropriate to seek justice and fairness in the resolution of the divorce-related issues. But justice and fairness are not, themselves, void of respect and mutual acceptance, for true justice would imply that neither spouse would be unjustly deprived or treated. True fairness would require that the parties making the agreement would need to seek to understand the needs, hopes, and desires of the other.

In a theological sense, justice is that which is in conformity with the will of God. The search for justice is based on determining which of competing values deserves the highest priority, requiring the parties to put themselves in the shoes of the other in order to understand the other's hopes and fears. It is my experience that justice is best achieved when the parties approach each other looking for understanding and respect. But if that is not possible, the search for a fair resolution of the issues is often a first step toward what may, later, become reconciliation.

Naming the Experience

To put a name to the transcendent experience in mediation is to name that which most characterizes God's presence for the divorcing couple. Some people identify the sense of caring, respect, and dignity that often emerges in mediation as the presence of God. Others name it as something they achieved personally, without acknowledging the mystery that is part of the process.

Others experience a sense of shalom or peace. For some this may mean simply the absence of war, the end of battle, the release that comes when the struggle is over. For others, however, mediation brings them closer to their divorcing spouse or their children. They experience a sense of being heard, understood, and accepted. Their shalom is a deeply felt experience in which they feel a gap has been bridged between themselves and another.

On one hand, the mediator's objective is to assist the divorcing couple in reaching agreement by resolving differences as amicably as possible. On the other hand, it is always hoped that the process of mediation will also help couples learn to resolve differences more easily and to improve communications. When divorcing spouses not only reach agreement but also experience the desire to help the other begin to recover from the divorce itself, they have fully experienced God's presence in a real and meaningful way.

Conclusion

Mediation is most successful when the participants and their children experience God's unconditional love. Through that love they can establish new relationships among themselves and with God. Since no specific professional category of pastoral mediator exists as of this writing, divorcing couples who wish to use this unique approach to divorce may have to consult with a mediator with the kind of integrity that would make him or her sensitive to the religious and spiritual dimensions inherent in such a process, or secure pastoral support throughout the process with a trusted minister or religious counselor.

God's grace abounds when no harm comes to either the couple or to the children and dignity is maintained during the divorce process. The sweetest thing the mediator can hear when the final agreement is reached is that the spouses respect and care for one another, even though they know that they cannot live together as husband and wife.

Dignity can be defined in several ways. The definition that best expresses the hope of mediation is the acknowledgment of the worth of a person or thing. If couples can survive the divorce transition with a sense of worth, both for themselves and for each other, then it can be said that God has been present. Mediation, like so much of life, is most successful when the spiritual is woven into the fabric of our very real lives.

Chapter 8

Where Do We Begin?

Begin by deciding it's worth a try. There is little to lose and much to gain. Regardless of where the couple is in the divorce or legal separation process, it is never too late to begin mediation.

For some people, bringing up the subject of mediation is the hardest part. For others, it is simply a matter of talking with their spouse. Raise the subject, talk with each other about it, discuss what you know about it:

— mediation is voluntary
— there is no obligation
— it is not necessary to hire or fire attorneys
— the participants never lose the option of resuming or beginning an adversarial approach
— the intent of mediation is to reach agreement and avoid costly litigation and unnecessary pain and anguish.

Special Circumstances

It is not unusual for one spouse to want mediation and the other to resist it, at least initially. But because mediation is a neutral approach, the resistant spouse will often come to accept mediation, even if that spouse is still unwilling to discuss other issues.

If there is no communication between you, or the communication is strained, the mediator might help get mediation started. Sometimes the mere fact that the suggestion to mediate comes from one divorcing partner makes the other resistant to the idea. When the resistant spouse talks with the mediator, he or she is often able to see the benefits of a mediated approach. I have dealt with many cases in which one spouse simply told the other about mediation, and then the resistant spouse called me or I called the spouse. The phone call paved the way for an initial mediation session.

Find a Mediator

The second step is to find a mediator. Ask around. Check with people you trust: A family counselor. A close friend. A minister or religious leader. Look up mediation in the Yellow Pages. Mediators are out there, ready to help.

Another approach to finding a mediator is to contact one of the mediation associations listed in the Appendix. The Academy of Family Mediators is a professional association of mediators that promotes standards of professional practice and training. The AFM can provide the names of mediators by state and city as well as basic information about mediation.

Ask questions. Who is the mediator? What is the mediator's educational background and work experience? Is he or she a member of appropriate professional organizations? How many years has the person been in mediation practice? Is the mediator a lawyer or a mental health professional? Is his or her practice primarily mediation, or is it simply an adjunct to other professional work? How much does it cost? What happens if . . . ? To develop a trusting relationship, it is important to know as much as you can about the professional who will become intimately involved in resolving your disputes.

Talk with the Mediator

For many people, it is important to have a conversation with the mediator before setting an appointment. It is often a good idea for both spouses to talk with the mediator. Sometimes one spouse feels that the mediator is biased because the other spouse talked with the mediator first. If both call, this misconception can be easily dispelled.

It is appropriate to explore the mediator's range of applicable information by asking pointed questions. Does the mediator demonstrate basic knowledge of pension plans, for example, and the tax effects of child and spousal support? What about child custody? Has the mediator worked with people who are moving to different states? How does spousal or child support work? The mediator need not be an expert in all of these areas but should have a working knowledge sufficient to assist the divorcing couple in reaching agreement or to direct them to appropriate experts.

A divorcing couple must have confidence in their mediator. As the number of mediators grows, so does their range of expertise and experience. Many have had excellent education and training. Some have practiced law or counseling or come to mediation with other valuable skills. More pastors and pastoral counselors are developing skills as divorce mediators.

However, as mediation grows in popularity, couples need to exercise caution. One woman said that her therapist agreed to be their mediator if they wished to take that approach to their divorce. "After all," the woman told me, "she said she had been in personnel work before becoming a therapist."

Get a Sense of the Mediator's Skill

Some divorcing couples find it helpful to call several mediators and compare responses to get a sense of each one's level of experience, skill, and competency. In some areas of the country, it may not be possible to find more than one mediator. Where possible, however, comparing price, experience, and expertise can improve the chances of successful mediation.

Calling the mediator is a valuable way to determine the mediator's accessibility. Did you reach the mediator quickly? Did the mediator return your call promptly? Was he or she friendly, supportive, and informative on the phone? Not only is it heartening for a mediator to know that you chose him or her on the basis of the initial phone conversation, it also lets the mediator know that you will be taking the mediation seriously.

Prepare for Your First Appointment

An ideal way to prepare for the first mediation appointment is to anticipate questions that need to be addressed. Divorce is difficult. Often, divorcing spouses are facing issues and concerns they have not had to deal with before: finances, capital gains taxes, monthly budgets, investment of funds. It can be overwhelming to cope with high emotions, come to grips with the important issues, make sense out of an uncertain future, and deal with the pain of the transition all at the same time.

It is often helpful for the divorcing couple to sift through the issues they are facing to assure that each issue is dealt with in the proper forum. Emotional issues are best dealt with through individual counseling or therapy. A tax expert is best consulted for questions about the tax implications of divorce. A real estate agent can be of help in dealing with real property. A lawyer can give advice about legal rights, duties, and obligations.

Often the arenas get confused, causing undue stress and delay. The most frequent confusion arises when the adversarial legal process is used to work out emotional or relationship issues. This is both costly and damaging. When in doubt, use mediation to discuss the problem and come to a mutually agreeable settlement.

When possible, reach as much agreement as possible before coming to mediation. However, do not consider any agreement final until you have full and complete knowledge of all that is involved. You should not let pre-mediation discussions turn into arguments and conflict. If arguments start, wait until the next mediation session before pursuing the issue. There you can explore the problems safely with the help of a neutral third party.

Recognize the Emotionality of Divorce

Frequently, couples come to mediation angry because one spouse made an initial promise and later retracted that promise. Such was the case with the following couple.

Stan and Lois

When Stan and Lois first talked about divorce, Stan said that Lois and the children would not have to leave the family home. Stan was well-intentioned when he made this promise to Lois. As time went on, however, it became clear to Stan that there would not be enough money to support two households, cover school tuition for the children, and still keep the family residence. He suggested that they sell the house.

Lois could not believe her ears. She was angry and upset about the possibility of selling the house. It was as if Stan were "pulling the rug out from under me and the kids," as Lois angrily put it.

Making promises to one another early in the process sometimes means that the promises must later be broken. Divorce is an emotional process; couples will often say things in the heat of an argument or out of hurt and pain—or in an attempt to be fair or compassionate—that will later be changed. After several mediation sessions, Stan and Lois were able to explore together the implications of keeping or selling the house and to decide on a course of action they could both accept.

Come to Mediation with an Open Mind

One of the most common statements made by couples after mediation is that through the process they had dealt with issues they had not even considered beforehand. A trained, experienced mediator will be sure the couple discusses all the issues important to their circumstances: college education, tax liability for the years of the marriage, life insurance to protect support payments, co-parenting concerns such as notification in case of illness, and changes in locations, to name a few.

Come Prepared Neither to Win nor Lose

The adversarial approach to divorce is frequently referred to as a "win-lose" approach. The decision goes either for or against an individual. This approach encourages a win-at-all-costs mentality that is dangerous and at times can be vicious. Comparing mediation with the traditional adversarial approach, the *Wall Street Journal* (9 Sept. 1991) quoted a mediation participant as saying, "Lawyers want too much justice. I didn't want justice. I wanted to get it over with."

The mediation approach is often described as "win-win," expressing the hope that the resulting agreements are best for the divorcing individuals and their children. Describing mediation as win-win still promotes the need to win, however; it fails to acknowledge the deep pain that divorce causes for all those involved. People do not choose to divorce because it makes them happy; they choose divorce because it is better than the emotional suffocation or psychological death brought on by the breakdown of the marriage relationship.

Mediation is best described as surviving with as much dignity as possible. While most couples experience a sense of relief and understanding when they reach agreement, most wish divorce were not necessary in the first place.

Give the Process Your Best Shot

Mediation will be as successful as the participants are willing to let it be. A mediator cannot create love where there is hate, compassion where there is revenge, or agreement when the parties refuse to agree. Couples must be willing to be flexible and understanding, open to hearing and giving. With your mediator's help, you *can* let go of the hurt and pain that have guided your thoughts and actions. You can perceive the divorce transition as the first step toward building a new relationship based on acceptance, not judgment and fear.

Trust the mediation process, especially if you are having a hard time trusting each other. The process is structured to bring couples carefully and gently to agreement.

All too often, a spouse who is used to controlling the outcome of marital events and decisions wants to force things along. It takes great effort for such a person to let the other spouse become equally involved in decision-making. Sometimes the reverse is also true: One spouse has difficulty taking responsibility for decision-making, especially when this has not been the pattern in the relationship. It is important for both spouses to feel that they are contributing to the flow of the mediation, that things will not proceed without them.

Conclusion

It was your marriage. Make it your divorce. Go through it together. Work with one another. Seek to keep control of how you choose to divorce. The more you relinquish control of the process, the harder it is to maintain dignity.

Years ago, when I was facing divorce myself, a friend commented on the dilemma he felt as he watched me go through this life transition: "One doesn't say congratulations and one doesn't say condolences. All I can say is, I hope you're happier."

Mediation does not celebrate the divorce, nor does it lament the demise of the marriage. Mediation provides a way of getting through the divorce so that the divorcing couple will have a better chance of finding the happiness they seek and experiencing the dignity they deserve.

Appendix
Mediation Organizations

Academy of Family Mediators
P.O. Box 10501
Eugene, OR 97440
(503) 345-1205
Fax (503) 345-4024

American Arbitration Association
140 West 51st Street
New York, NY 10020-1203
(212) 484-4000

American Bar Association
Family Law/Mediation Section
750 North Lake Shore Drive
Chicago, IL 60611
(312) 988-5000

Association of Family and Conciliation Courts
329 West Wilson
Madison, WI 53703
(608) 251-4001

References

Berman, Harold. 1974. *The Interaction of Law and Religion*. Nashville: Abingdon Press.

Cobb, John B. 1977. *Theology and Pastoral Care*. Philadelphia: Fortress Press.

David, René. 1972. *Les grands systemes de droit contemporains*. Paris: Précis Dalloz.

Folberg, Jay, and Alison Taylor. 1985. *Mediation*. San Francisco: Jossey-Bass.

Gannett News Service. 14 May 1991. "Study: Kids of Divorce Tend to Repeat Split." *Independent Journal* (Novato, Calif.).

Kelly, Joan B. 1990. "Is Mediation Less Expensive? Comparison of Mediated and Adversarial Divorce Costs." *Mediation Quarterly* 8, no. 1:15–26.

Lemmon, John A., ed. 1991. Special issue on international developments in mediation. *Mediation Quarterly* 8, no. 4.

Melamed, James. Spring 1989. "Attorneys and Mediation: From Threat to Opportunity." *Mediation Quarterly* 23:13–22.

Pearson, Jessica, and Nancy Thoennes. 1982. "The Benefits Outweigh the Costs." *Family Law Advocate* 4:26–32.

———. 1984. "Mediating and Litigating Custody Disputes:

A Longitudinal Evaluation."*Family Law Quarterly* 17:479–524.

Sapoznek, David. 1983. *Mediating Child Custody Disputes.* San Francisco: Jossey-Bass.

Smedes, Lewis B. 1984. *Forgive and Forget: Healing the Hurts We Don't Deserve.* San Francisco: Harper & Row.

Teilhard de Chardin, Pierre. 1974. *On Suffering.* New York: Harper & Row.

Wall Street Journal. 9 Sept. 1991. "Mediators Thrive Heading Off Lawsuits: Push to Avoid Costly Litigation Spawns a Boom." Enterprise section.

Wallerstein, Judith S., and Sandra Blakeslee. 1987. *Second Chances: Men, Women and Children a Decade After Divorce.* New York: Ticknor & Fields.

Weitzman, Lenore J. 1985. *The Divorce Revolution: The Unexpected Social and Economic Consequences for Women and Children in America.* New York: The Free Press.

Select Bibliography

Berman, Harold. *The Interaction of Law and Religion.* Nashville: Abingdon Press, 1974.

Blades, Joan. *Family Mediation: Cooperative Divorce Settlement.* Englewood Cliffs, N.J.: Prentice-Hall, 1985.

Clinebell, Howard J., Jr. *Basic Types of Pastoral Counseling.* Nashville: Abingdon Press, 1966.

David, René. *Les grands systemes de droit contemporains.* Paris: Précis Dalloz, 1972.

Folberg, Jay, and Alison Taylor. *Mediation.* San Francisco: Jossey-Bass, 1985.

Hanson, Freya Ottem, and Terje C. Hanson. *Mediation for Troubled Marriages.* Minneapolis: Augsburg Press, 1989.

Kelly, Joan B. "Is Mediation Less Expensive? Comparison of Mediated and Adversarial Divorce Costs." *Mediation Quarterly* 8, no. 1 (1990):15–26.

Lemmon, John A., ed. Special issue on international developments in mediation. *Mediation Quarterly* 8, no. 4 (1991).

Melamed, James. "Attorneys and Mediation: From Threat to Opportunity." *Mediation Quarterly* 23 (Spring 1989):13–22.

Moore, Christopher. *The Mediation Process: Practical*

Strategies for Resolving Conflict. San Francisco: Jossey-Bass, 1986.

Pearson, Jessica, and Nancy Thoennes. "The Benefits Outweigh the Costs." *Family Law Advocate* 4 (1982):26–32.

————. "Mediating and Litigating Custody Disputes: A Longitudinal Evaluation." *Family Law Quarterly* 17 (1984):479–524.

Rambo, Lewis R. *The Divorcing Christian.* Nashville: Abingdon Press, 1983.

Ricci, Isolina. *Mom's House, Dad's House.* New York: Collier Books, 1980.

Sapoznek, David. *Mediating Child Custody Disputes.* San Francisco: Jossey-Bass, 1983.

Smedes, Lewis B. *Forgive and Forget: Healing the Hurts We Don't Deserve.* San Francisco: Harper & Row, 1984.

Teilhard de Chardin, Pierre. *On Suffering.* New York: Harper & Row, 1974.

Wallerstein, Judith S., and Sandra Blakeslee. *Second Chances: Men, Women and Children a Decade After Divorce.* New York: Ticknor & Fields, 1987.

Wallerstein, Judith, and Joan B. Kelly. *Surviving the Breakup: How Children and Parents Cope with Divorce.* New York: Basic Books, 1980.

Weitzman, Lenore J. *The Divorce Revolution: The Unexpected Social and Economic Consequences for Women and Children in America.* New York: The Free Press, 1985.